A

PRACTICAL THEORY

OF

VOUSSOIR ARCHES.

BY

PROF. WILLIAM CAIN, C. E.

NEW YORK:
D. VAN NOSTRAND, PUBLISHER,
23 MURRAY AND 27 WARREN STREET.
1874.

PREFACE.

The following little treatise first appeared in VAN NOSTRAND'S ENGINEERING MAGAZINE, for which it was written. The author hopes that he may be doing a service to American readers in introducing to them Dr. Scheffler's Theory of Arches, the fundamental principles of which are contained in the following pages. Vertical forces alone are considered. Numerous experiments are given in illustration of the theory advanced, both for symmetrical arches as well as for unsymmetrical arches, or arches unsymmetrically loaded. It is believed that the following theory is easily acquired, is rapid in working and agrees with experiment, and therefore can properly be called "A Practical Theory of Voussoir Arches."

WM. CAIN.

A PRACTICAL THEORY OF VOUSSOIR ARCHES.

1. The theory selected, in the following treatise, is that of Dr. Hermann Scheffler, * which will be quoted from literally in places. A sufficient number of experiments with wooden arches, probably to establish this theory, will also be given.

It is necessary to consider *the principle of the least resistance* in order that the thrust, anywhere in an arch, in direction, position and magnitude, may be located.

The Rev. Canon Mosely is the author

* Detailed in his most excellent German work, a French translation of which by M. Victor Fournie is entitled "Traitê de la Stabilitė des constructions; 1re partie, Theorie des Voutes et des Murs de Soutênement." Paris, 1864.

of this principle, which has been amplified by Dr. Scheffler in his treatise above alluded to. It may be briefly stated thus :

Principle of the least resistance. Let the external forces which act upon a structure, be combined into one resultant, P ; and let the resisting forces R′, R′′ - - - be each decomposed into components respectively ⊥ and ∥ to the direction of P. Then will the components of R′, R′′ - - - - ⊥ to P be the least that will cause equilibrium, consistently with the physical properties of the body or bodies composing the structure. *For* the sum of the components ∥ to P must equal P ; but the components ⊥ to P are only brought into play from the peculiar disposition of the resisting surfaces of the structure and there is no need for their further increase after they have caused stability.

As M. Fournie observes : This supposes *first*, "that the *molecular* actions, which constitute the reactions, take place without sensible velocity ;" *secondly*, "that the *molecular* actions are developed successively : so that the system cannot arrive at the position of greatest tensions without having passed through the positions of less tensions. Constructors willingly admit these propositions as plausible. The principle follows immediately."

Example. * Let a beam, as in Fig. 1, lean against a horizontal wall at A and a vertical wall at B; its extremities may slide on those planes, requiring friction to prevent it. The weight P of the beam acts through its centre of gravity, and by the above principle, if the resultant resistances at A and B be decomposed into vertical and horizontal components : the sum of the vertical components=P and the horizontal components must be the smallest that the friction, between the walls and beam, will admit of : hence the directions of the resistances $F_1 R_2$ and $F_1 R_1$ must be as near the vertical as possible. But with regard to the physical disposition of the surfaces AE and BE, it is necessary to equilibrium that the directions of R and R_1 make angles with

* "Traité de la Stabilité," § 5.

the normals to BE and AE, at most, equal to the angles of friction ϕ_2, ϕ_1, of

FIG. 1.

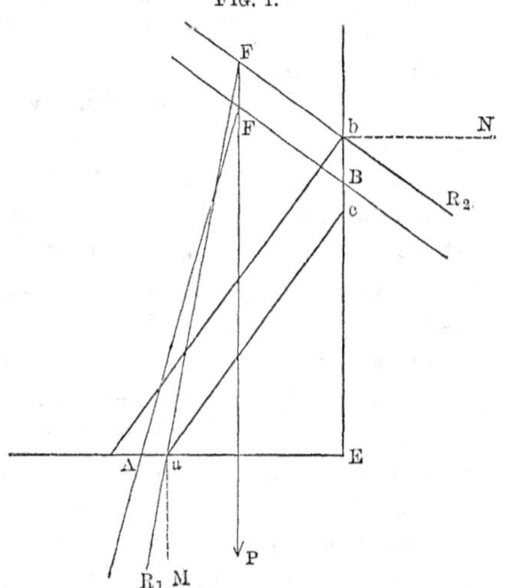

the ends of the beam on those planes : hence take $R_2\ b\ N = \phi_2$ which gives the direction of R_2. As the direction of R_1 must intersect that of R_2 on P : we have $F_1\ R_1$ the direction of R_1.

It is evident that for incompressible voussoirs, the force R_2 passes through *b* and R_1 through *a*, as this gives the least horizontal thrust; the directions of R_1 and R_2 being more nearly vertical than when they pass throug hany other points, as A and B.

For an elastic, compressible beam; as it will bend as well as compress at the edges, the force R_2 will pass near edge *c*, and the force R_1 near edge *a*.

If by the construction above, $R_1 a M$ becomes $> \phi_1$ the beam will fall by sliding. The molecular resistances at A and B act along a portion of the surfaces *bc*, *a*A, for compressible beams, though they vary in intensity so that their resultants pass near the edges *c* and *a*. For the mere supposititious case of an incompressible beam, the resultants pass through the edges, and hence there is but one molecular force acting on a mathematical point at either *b* or *a*. An experimental proof of this theory will be given in Art. 10.

Most writers *assume* the force R_2 as horizontal, which is evidently only the case when there is no friction between the beam and the vertical wall. This is among the untrue hypotheses that are often so confidently stated by learned mathematicians.

SYMMETRICAL ARCHES.

FIG. 2.

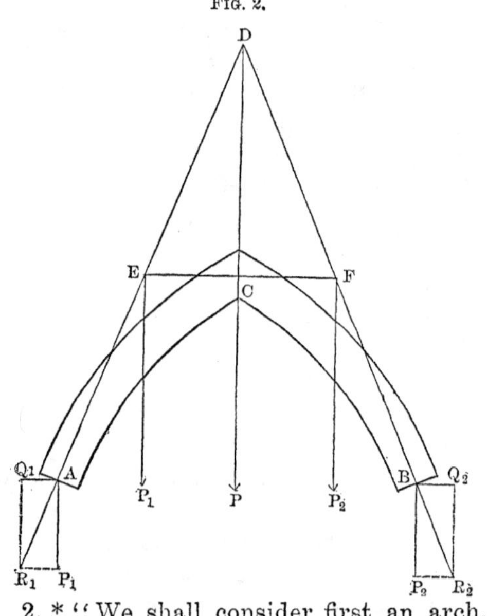

2. * "We shall consider first an arch,

* § 8.

formed of two branches AC, BC, (Fig. 2), symmetrical and placed in juxtaposition, and comprised between two parallel vertical planes ⊥ to axis of arch," the arch being right cylindrical. "This arch, composed of voussoirs in the shape of wedges, formed of *incompressible* materials, leans against two abutments at its extremities A and B, and is loaded not only with its own weight but with any other weight whatsoever, distributed symmetrically on either side of the crown C. The mass of the arch is subject to the laws of friction in its joints. The adherence of the mortar, interposed between the voussoirs, being difficult to estimate will not be considered." As the two half arches are symmetrical as to the crown C, it is clear that the points of application, A and B of the reactions R_1 and R_2 of the surfaces of support, will be also symmetrical in relation to the vertical passing through the crown, and that the line AB will be horizontal, in whatsoever manner the points A and B may vary upon the surfaces of support.

If we decompose the reactions, R_1 and R_2, into their horizontal and vertical components P_1, Q_1, P_2, Q_2, we should have $P_1 = P_2 =$ the weight of half arch with its load, and the thrust $Q_1 = Q_2$, should from the principle of the least resistance be a minimum.

Let us consider now one of the two halves, for example AC. Let EP_1 be the vertical passing through the centre of gravity of this half with its load ; to hold this mass in equilibrium it is necessary that there exist at the crown a force whose direction CE passes through the point of intersection E of the vertical EP_1 with the direction of the reaction R_1.

As the vertical component of R_1 equals the weight P_1 acting through E, we conclude, without difficulty, that the tension at the crown C of the arch is necessarily equal to the second component Q_1, of the reaction R_1 and must be horizontal as it is.

From what precedes we are allowed to consider only a half-arch, leant against a fixed surface at A, and solicited by a horizontal force at C. When there is equilibrium, we shall seek the least value of this horizontal force Q and its point of application at the crown.

Fig. 3.

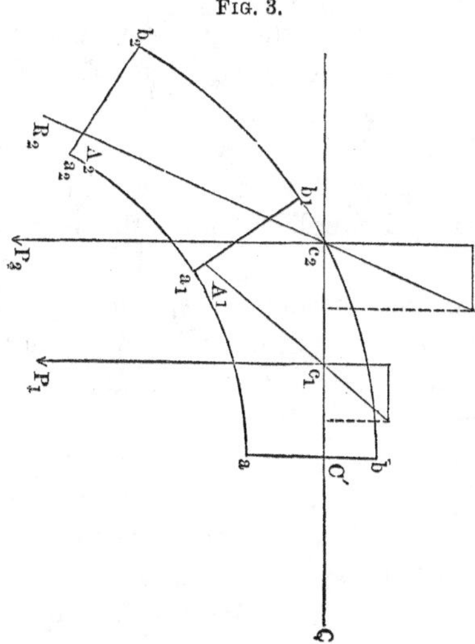

3. (Fig 3). Let ab, a_1b_1, a_2b_2, be the joints of an arch; P_1, P_2, the vertical directions of the weights of the parts $ab\ b_1a_1$; $abb_2\ a_2$; including the loads on the parts bb_1, b_1b_2, ... ; P_1,P_2 acting through the centres of gravity of the parts considered.

The horizontal force Q combined with the reaction R_2 at the joint a_2b_2 holds the part abb_2a_2 in equilibrium and similarly for the reactions on other joints.

At the points where the direction of Q cuts P_1, P_2, combine those forces with Q, the resultant of Q and P_1 cuts joints a_1b_1 at A_1, which is therefore the *centre of pressure* on that joint. As the weight abb_2a_2 with its load equals P_2 and is the weight on joints a_2 b_2, the resultant of P_2 and Q will give the force acting on a_2b_2 in direction, position and magnitude; its direction cuts a_2b_2 at A_2, which is therefore the *centre of pressure* on that joint.

In the same way the resultants and centres of pressure on all the joints may be determined. A broken line connecting these *centres of pressure* on the various joints is called by Dr. Scheffler the *line of pressures.* For voussoirs indefinitely small it becomes a curved line.

That granted, in order that the arch may remain in equilibrium, it is necessary:

1. That the points of intersection C′, A_1, A_2, fall in the interior of the respective joints

ab, a_1b_1, a_2b_2. If for any joint this is not so, *e.g.*, if the point A_1 was above b_1, the mass abb_1a_1 would then turn around the edge b_1, as an unresisted couple would be formed. To explain: suppose the resultant R_1 to pass outside of joint a_1b_1; conceive two equal opposed forces, each equal to R_3 to act at edge b_1; this does not disturb the equilibrium; then R_1 the force acting through A_1 (which is outside the joint) with its equal but not directly opposed force at b_1, would form the unresisted couple in question which causes overturning.

2. That the directions c_1A_1, c_2A_2 of the pressures upon the joints do not make angles, with the normals to the respective joints which exceed the angle of friction. If it was not so, sliding at the joints in question would occur of the mass above or below.

However, the friction of the materials usually employed in construction is sufficiently great to not give cause for fear as regards sliding, generally.

It is very easy to alter the direction of

the joints should sliding be apprehended, hence it will not be considered further.

It is to be remarked that the foregoing theory does not require horizontal resistance in the spandrel, which is not generally built with the same care that is taken in the construction of the arch stones, and hence cannot generally be regarded as unyielding; hence when a *line of pressures* such as $CA_1 A_2$ passes, somewhere, out of the arch ring, a serious derangement of the arch may occur, even though the spandrel may prevent its falling: hence it appears to be a poor construction, to build such an arch, in preference to an arch in which the resultant pressures on the joints everywhere keep within the limits of the arch ring. This will be adverted to again.

4. It is necessary to demonstrate a few propositions, to locate the true line of pressures, corresponding to the minimum of the horizontal thrust.

The voussoirs will be considered indefinitely small; hence the line, drawn through the centres of pressure at each joint, will be a curved line, which is probably what it is in real arches, with voussoirs of any size. As before remarked, Dr. Scheffler calls this line, the *line of pressures.*

None of the joints will be supposed to make angles to the left of the vertical, looking upwards, greater than 90°

*(See Fig. 4.) If we vary at will the greatness and point of application of the horizontal force Q at the crown, we obtain curves which mutually cut each other. *But two such curves, which cut each other in any point whatsoever, D, will cut each other only at points situated upon the same horizontal as D; otherwise they will not meet again in any point above or below this horizontal.*

To demonstrate these propositions, let P_1 be the weight which corresponds to the *joint* that the curve of pressures traverses at the point D. Let $p_1 =$ distance of the point D from the vertical through the centre of gravity of the weight P_1.

The moment of P_1 in relation to D is thus $P_1 p_1$. If Q is the horizontal pressure at C and z the depth of the point D below

---

*p. 34.

the horizontal through the point C, zQ is the moment of Q as to D ; D being a point of the curve of pressures.

FIG. 4.

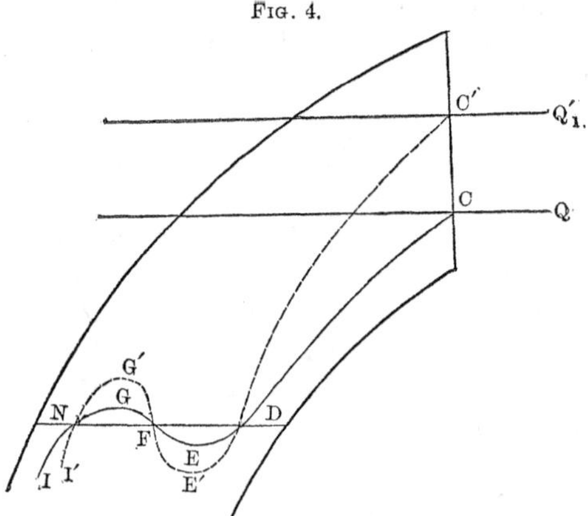

We have the characteristic relation, $zQ = P_1 p_1$. Let F be another point of the same curve at the *same height* as D. Let P_2, p_2, be the weight and lever arm, corresponding to the point F: $zQ = P_2 p_2$ whence $P_1 p_1 = P_2 p_2$.

If now a new curve of pressures is supposed to pass through D; ($z_2 Q_2 = P_2 p_2$) and consequently $z_1 Q_1 = P_2 p_2$; hence it passes through F and cuts the first curve on the same horizontal as D_1.

Next let there be I, a point of the first curve which is not at the same height as the point D; P_3 the weight on the joint which passes through I; p_3 the distance from I to the vertical through the centre of gravity of this weight and h, the difference of level between I and D. We have for all curves, which pass through these two points.

$$z\,Q = p_1P_1 \text{ and } (h + z)\,Q = p_3P_3$$

whence

$$Q = \frac{p_3P_3 - p_1P_1}{h} \text{ and } z = \frac{p_1P_1h}{p_3P_3 - p_1P_1}$$

according to which, while h has a finite value, Q and z have necessarily *fixed values*, which can correspond but to a single curve of pressures.

Hence two different curves can never cut each other in two points situated at different heights. It may be remarked that isolated weights may produce curves of pressure like either of those drawn in Fig. 4, though such curves are but rarely met with in practice.

The meeting of two curves at C′, E, G,—with a horizontal tangent is a contact and not an intersection; as we can consider the contact of the two curves as the coincidence of two points indefinitely near on the same level. For points, such as D, which have no horizontal tangent, the meeting is an intersection and not a contact from the same consideration.

In fact suppose for an instant that the dotted curve has contact only with the first at E. Suppose now the value of Q_1 to diminish from a change in the point of application of the thrust at the abutment. From a consideration of Fig. 3 we see that the curve will move down the joint, to the right of E, and hence must cut the first to the right of E and above it. Its other intersections, it has just been shown are at F, N - - at the same level as D, the first point of crossing.

These important propositions being established, the problem before us is the following: Among all the curves of pressure, possible, which lie in the arch ring, find that for which the thrust Q is a minimum, and which by the principle of the least resistance is the only true one.

5. (See Fig. 5.) Proposition :—*When the point F, of contact with the extrados, is higher than the point of contact E, with the intrados, of a curve of pressures; it corresponds to the minimum of the thrust, whether the point E, precedes or follows the point F, going along the curve from the crown to the abutment.*

Fig. 5 represents the last mentioned case, which is the most usual; the other, being very rarely found in practice, will not be demonstrated. The case represented by Fig. 5 is demonstrated as follows:

1. If preserving the point of application K, we augment or diminish the thrust Q, the curve will either go outside of the extrados at F or the intrados at E, and hence will be impossible. This is easily seen from the construction of Fig. 3, where a greater horizontal thrust moves the points A_1, A_2 - - nearer the extrados, a less thrust toward the intrados.

2. If preserving the force Q, we raise its points of application towards D, we obtain

a new curve, which is entirely above the first, which cuts then the extrados about

FIG. 5.

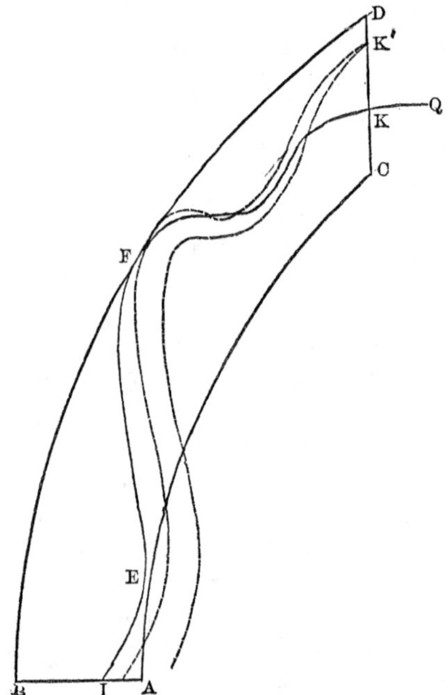

the point F: it is then impossible. This may also readily be seen by a consideration of Fig. 3. If now we augment Q, the curve will be raised still higher near F and, of course, will go out of the arch ring and thus be less possible.

3. If, however, with the point of application still above K, at K^1 for example, we diminish Q so that the part of the curve near F may become tangent to the extrados, it is necessary that this new curve cuts the first K F E I *somewhere* between F and K. By Art. 4, as F is below K, this intersection may take place in a single point (lower dotted line), or according to the particular form of the curve in an odd number of points on the same horizontal (upper dotted line); so that, in all cases the new curve will be to the right of the first curve between F and the nearest point of intersection, but as below this last point the curve cannot meet again the first, it will remain constantly to the right of it; hence it will cut the intrados near E. It is then impossible. There cannot exist then a curve, under the assumed conditions, meeting the crown joint in a point higher than K.

4. If now we lower the point K without changing Q, the curve will cut the intrados above E, as it must remain below and to the right of the first curve; and for a stronger reason if Q is diminished. But if we increase the value of Q, in this new point of application below K, sufficiently, the curve may remain entirely in the interior of the arch, and generally an indefinite number of curves of pressure can be drawn in the arch. From what precedes, it follows that the curve K F E I, corresponds to the minimum of Q, since for the point K there is only one curve, for a point above K, there cannot exist a curve, and for a lower point, there are only curves corresponding to greater values of Q.

It will frequently happen that F coincides with D, and E with A ; in which cases the meeting of the curves with the extrados or the intrados is not necessarily a contact. The preceding demonstrations nevertheless hold.

6. When the point of contact F with the extrados is lower than the point E of the intrados, the curve of pressures corresponds to the maximum of the thrust Q.

It would be foreign to the purpose of this article to demonstrate this; (which is however easily done in the manner just shown; and in the same way the other case of the minimum is easily demonstrated) or to give all the cases where rupture occurs, which Dr. Scheffler has so fully illustrated.

Suffice it to say that the whole theory of curves of pressure is solved by him as simply as artistically. As he remarks: * "An exact knowledge of the actions that are produced in an arch can alone give to the constructor the proper confidence to design the form of an arch, the thickness of the arch, the joints, and the abutments in such a manner as to assure the stability of all the parts; and this is especially true of a new work, where experience and analogy do not furnish the needed information."

Numerous experiments will be given in the sequel, which will be found to agree with this theory, and to establish it practically, taking into consideration the compressibility of the materials used.

---

* p. 193.

7. Before going further, it would be as well, perhaps, to make some remarks about the effects produced by the compressibility of the voussoirs and mortar. As the law of that compressibility is unknown, we can not tell exactly how far from the

FIG. 6.

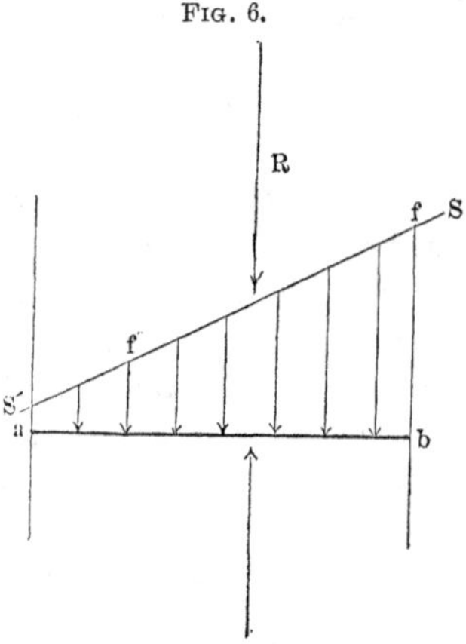

edges of the joints is the nearest approach of the curve of pressures in an arch. It may be kept in view though that the resultant pressure on any joint, can be exactly at the edge of the joint only for *incompressible voussoirs* that can receive a finite effort upon a mathematical line. For actual bodies, this finite force must be distributed over a finite surface.

Let the molecular reactions, which make up the resultant on each joint, be supposed parallel in direction. Conceive a plane passing through the resultant R (Fig. 6) on any joint, parallel to the intrados at the joint in question.

Call an *elementary resisting force* on one side of this plane f, and its lever arm in relation to that plane l. Likewise call f' and l' an elementary force, and its lever arm on the other side of this plane; then we must always have

$$\Sigma f\,l = \Sigma f'\,l'$$

It is evident that if at any joint the resultant passes near an edge b, that Σf is much greater than $\Sigma f',$ as the last forces act with greater lever arms; hence in any actual arch the resultant falls back a certain distance from the edge necessarily on account of the greater compression produced at that edge; and this is moreover necessary to prevent crushing, as our materials are not infinitely strong.

For example, in the head of the bridge of Neuilly, the horizontal thrust at the crown on a slice 1ft. in thickness is about 109 tons, supposing the line of pressures to pass through the upper edge of crown joint. In reality it is at a certain distance from this edge, which if we knew as well as Σf between that distance and the edge, we could form a better idea as to whether the surface included was able to bear the thrust. Thus suppose in this case that $\Sigma f = \frac{3}{4} 109 = 82$ tons and on such a small surface as we shall find that it is uniformly distributed. If the crushing force of the stone is taken at five tons per sq. in, this would require a bearing surface of $82 \div 5 = 16$ sq. in.; *i.e.* the resultant could pass within 1.33 inches of the edge without causing rupture. Mortar has a much less crushing weight than good granite in blocks, but for a mortar joint only say $\frac{1}{8}$ inch thick, its crushing weight must approach that of some building stones, and probably the resultant could pass within 6 inches of the edge in this bridge without causing rupture. There are reported many cracks in the head of this bridge. It is very probable though that the resultant retreats farther in the arch ring, for swift rolling loads could then too readily crush the edges, as the molecular resistances take time to act and assume their final magnitude, the curve of pressure changing with every rolling load. Again, take the viaduct Fig. 9, which is 50ft. span and 10ft. rise; the horizontal thrust on 1ft. of thickness is 20 tons, which can be borne on a surface of 4 sq. in. by granite, the mortar requiring the line of pressures to retreat a few inches from the edge. The depth of the voussoirs at the crown in this bridge is 2.5ft.; for the bridge of Neuilly 5.3 feet; we thus see that the resultant *may* pass, proportionally to the depth of the voussoirs, very near the edge without causing crushing, and as on most bridges there is no crushing at the edges, we infer that this resultant must pass a certain distance from the edge in every instance.

The mortar may, besides giving a more intimate, and consequently a greater bearing surface, cause the line of pressures to retreat within the arch ring, thus distributing the thrust a little more uniformly over the joint. Suppose the centre of an arch struck as soon as it is turned, while the mortar is still fresh at the crown ; for the usual forms of bridge arches, the mortar will be compressed, and in fact squeezed partially out at the upper edges of the joints near the crown, and this will be the more marked the thicker the joints.

However, as the mortar hardens during the building of the spandrels, the line of pressure will afterwards approach the top of the crown joint as the arch is weighted down, any sinking of the crown being attended with a more intimate contact at the upper bearing surfaces at the crown. This becomes still more evident when we suppose a rolling load on the crown of an arch whose mortar joints have completely set, and likewise consider that the abutments yield slightly.

Shaving off the upper parts of the joints near the crown would tend to counteract this.

Dr. Scheffler thinks that, for good stone, if we can draw a line of pressures, within the arch, that nowhere approaches nearer the edges than $\frac{1}{4}$ depth of joint, that the stability of the arch is assured.

Dr. W. J. M. Rankine gives $\frac{1}{3}$ depth of joint as the nearest approach to the contour curves.

The experiments that will be given show very plainly that the total thrust on a joint, together with its special compressibility, alone locates the true curve of pressures, so that it will depend principally upon the dimensions of the arch and surcharge; for a small arch being very near the edges at the joints of rupture, for a larger arch with a greater thrust, at a greater distance from these edges.

It is a fact, in some existing arches, that the voussoirs at certain points are pressed together near their edges, the joints slightly opening on the other side.

At any rate wherever the engineer locates these circumscribing, limiting curves, to the curve of pressures, the latter must always conform to the minimum of the thrust in the limits chosen.

If no curve of pressure can be drawn in

the limits, the depth of the voussoirs must be increased on part or the whole of the arch; or the profile may be altered; or finally we may combine both of these methods to secure stability.

FIG. 7.

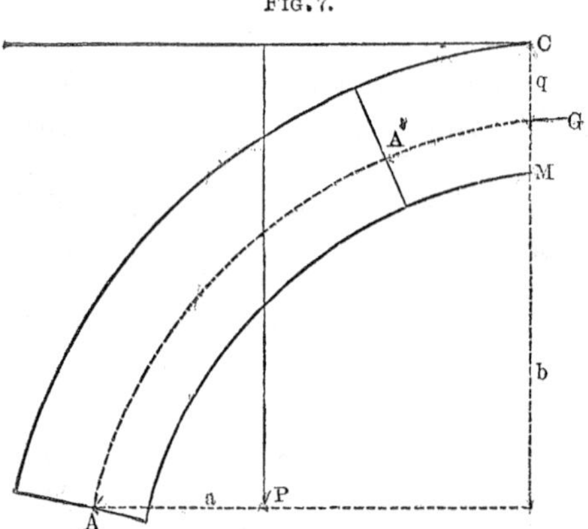

8. Let us consider as in Art. 2 a slice of the arch 1 unit thick. In Fig. 7, let Q= the horizontal thrust (compare Fig. 3 throughout); q, its vertical distance below the apex C; P=weight of an arch and load C A on joint at A; a=horizontal distance from A, the centre of pressure on the joint,

to the vertical passing through the centre of gravity, P ; h=vertical distance between C and A ; b=vertical distance between M, the point of application of Q at the crown, and A.

If we consider another point A′ of the curve of pressures, at a vertical distance above A=e, we shall have an analogous notation P_1, a_1, b_1.

If we know the points M and A, we have

$$a\,P = b\,Q \quad \therefore\ Q = \frac{a\,P}{b} \quad \ldots\ldots\ldots \quad (1).$$

If we know any two points as A, A′, $a\,P = b\,Q = (b' + e)\,Q$; also $a'\,P' = b'Q'$

hence
$$Q = \frac{P - a'\,P'}{e} \quad \ldots\ldots\ldots \quad (2)$$

$$q = h - \frac{a\,P}{Q} \quad \ldots\ldots\ldots\ldots \quad (3)$$

Having obtained from eq. (1) or eqs. (2) and (3), Q and its point of application at the crown, we find where the resultant pressures cut each joint as in Art 3, and if these points are within the proper limits of the arch ring and satisfy the minimum of the thrust, the curve is the true one. From eq. (1) it is evident that Q is smaller as b is greater or a smaller; hence the true curve will pass as near C, and the lowest point of the joint at A as the compressibility of the material will admit of.

If the first curve drawn, passes outside of the prescribed limits in one or more places; take points on the limiting curves opposite the points of maximum departure, and by eqs. (2) and (3), pass a curve through two of these points.

If the arch is stable at all, it will almost invariably be found in practice, that the last curve so drawn will fulfill the required conditions of remaining in the prescribed limits and corresponding to the minimum of the thrust. If not a third approximation may be tried, and so on.

In all the numerous and varied examples that Dr. Scheffler works out, he never resorts to a third trial; and in practice, after becoming familiar with the leading cases, the first trial is generally sufficient, when the limiting curves are assumed, as the writer can testify to from experience. Thus this theory does not demand an unlimited number of gropings as Poucelit asserts,* so

---

*Scheffler, p. 222,

as to render the method nearly illusory in practice.

Let us now proceed to show how to find the centres of gravity of the weights abb_1a_1, abb_2a_2, (Fig. 3), as also the magnitudes of those weights. If the arch is loaded with any weights, reduce them to the same specific gravity as that of the masonry of the bridge supposed homogeneous, as follows: Lay down these weights in their exact positions on the arch and alter the vertical dimensions to conform to the specific gravity of the stone. We shall thus substitute blocks of stones, by scale, for the surcharge of earth, water, etc., or the rolling load.

By this means we have the solid contents of abb_1a_1, etc., proportionate to the weights P_1, P_2 - - - and hence can be taken for them.

We now divide the horizontal through A (Fig 8) into an appropriate number of parts and through these points of division, draw verticals from the intrados to the curve DE that limits above the load.

Regard each trapezoid DGG′D′ as a

rectangle, and calculate its surface by multiplying its horizontal width AA′by the

Fig. 8.

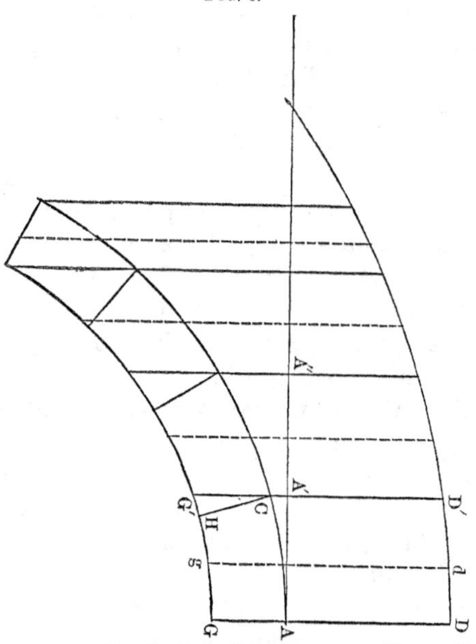

mean vertical *dg*. Next regarding the centre of gravity of each trapezoid as that of the corresponding rectangle, we shall find the centre of gravity of the trapezoid

DD′G′G, for example, to be upon the mean vertical *dg*. which equally divides the horizontal AA′. Draw through C, the joint CH; the weight DD′G′G will be considered as resting on the joint CH; which is in excess by the small triangle CG′H, an error too small to be regarded in flat arches.

There is, however, given by Dr. Scheffler, a very simple construction for a closer approximation to the truth. Further on will be indicated another method, which gives all desirable accuracy for any form of arch. In fact, considering that in practice arches are neither homogeneous nor symmetrical, perfect accuracy is not necessary, as there should be a margin left to allow for these variations always. In the case of the experiments with the wooden voussoirs, the writer has used a method which leaves nothing to be desired on the score of simplicity and accuracy.

Now if we multiply the surface of each trapezoid by the horizontal distance of its centre of gravity from A; the sum of these moments divided by the sum of the trapezoid surfaces (which are also the volumes), will give the horizontal distance from A to the centre of gravity of the whole part considered. This method will thus give us the weights P_1 P_2 - - - (Fig. 3), as well as the horizontal distance of their centres of gravity from the crown.

First Example.—Let us illustrate by an example of a railroad bridge (Fig. 9) of 50 ft. span and 10 ft. rise, the arch being a segment of a circle; voussoirs 2.5 deep; the spandrel walls rising 2.83 ft. above the summit of the arch ring. The arch is 7 ft. thick, but we shall consider but a vertical slice of it 1 ft. thick.

In the following table, the first column gives the number of the joint from the crown; the second (w) the width of the horizontal divisions AA′, A′A″- - of Fig. 8; the third (v) the corresponding mean heights *dg* - - -; the fourth (s), the product of these dimensions, giving thus the surface of each trapezoid. Column (c) gives the distances of the centre of gravity of each trapezoid from the crown; column (m) the product of (s) and (c).

Now we cumulate, giving from the crown in the next two columns these surfaces

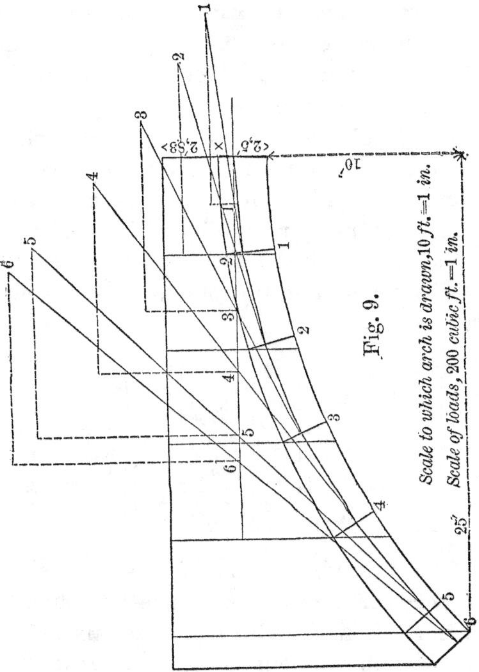

Fig. 9.

and products (s + c); column (S) being formed by adding the surface of each trapezoid to the total surface, just found, which precedes it. The last quantity in column (S) should = sum of column (s).

In the same way, column (M) contains the continued sum of column (m), and hence its last number should equal the sum of column (m). Dividing now the numbers in column (M) by the corresponding ones in column (S) we get, column (c), the horizontal distances of the centre of gravity of each weight P_1, P_2 — — corresponding to joists 1, 2 - - - from the crown.

	w	v	s	c	m	S	M	C
1	5	5.4	27.	2.5	67.50	27,	67.50	2.5
2	5	6.1	30.5	7.5	228.75	57.5	296.25	5.1
3	5	7.6	38.	12.5	475.	95.5	771.25	8.1
4	5	9.8	49.	17.5	857.50	144.5	1628.75	11.3
5	5	13.2	66.	22.5	1485.	210.5	3113.75	14.7
6	1.75	14.5	25.4	25.9	657.86	235.9	3771.61	16.
			235.9		3771,61			

The preceding table shows that the *surface* (or *content*, for a slice 1 ft. thick) of the half arch with its load equals 235.9 sq. ft.; its moment as to the crown is 3771.61 and the distance of its centre of gravity from the joint at the crown is 16 ft. Hence (see Fig. 7,) we have to pass a curve of pressures, through the crown joint, $\frac{1}{3}$ of its depth from the summit of the arch and through joint 6 at $\frac{1}{3}$ of its depth above its lowest point, if we decide on account of shocks due to passing loads, imperfection of workmanship, etc., to require that the curve of pressures shall not pass outside of the middle third of the arch ring. By measurement on the drawing (Fig. 9) we find a=25.6—16=9.6, b =11.2. We have also P=235.9 cubic feet of stone ; hence by formula (1)

$$Q=\frac{a\,P}{b}=\frac{235.9\times 9.6}{11.2}=202 \text{ cubic ft. stone}$$

which may be reduced to tons, when desired, by multiplying by the weight in tons of a cubic foot of stone.

If now at the points of intersection of the horizontal through the point of application of Q at the crown, with the verticals passing through the centres of gravity of the surfaces given in column (S), (P_1 P_2- - - of Fig. 3), the points of intersection, of the resultants of Q with these weights P_1, P_2.... with the corresponding joints, will be points in the curve of pressures sought.

For example, to determine where the line of pressures cuts joint 4, lay off the distance in column (C), 11.3 horizontally from the crown, then on a vertical lay off upward from this point the corresponding weight on joint 4, given in column (S) 144.5; drawing a horizontal line, through the last point found=Q, we get the resultant by completing the triangle of forces.

Producing this resultant to intersection with joint 4, will give the centre of pressure on that joint. It will be advisable, in practice, to prick off the centres of gravity, taken from column (C), at one operation and number each one with the number of the corresponding joint to avoid mistake.

On continuing this construction for each joint, we shall find that the line of pressures remains within the inner third of the arch ring.

It may be remarked that the small triangle mentioned is in excess only for the

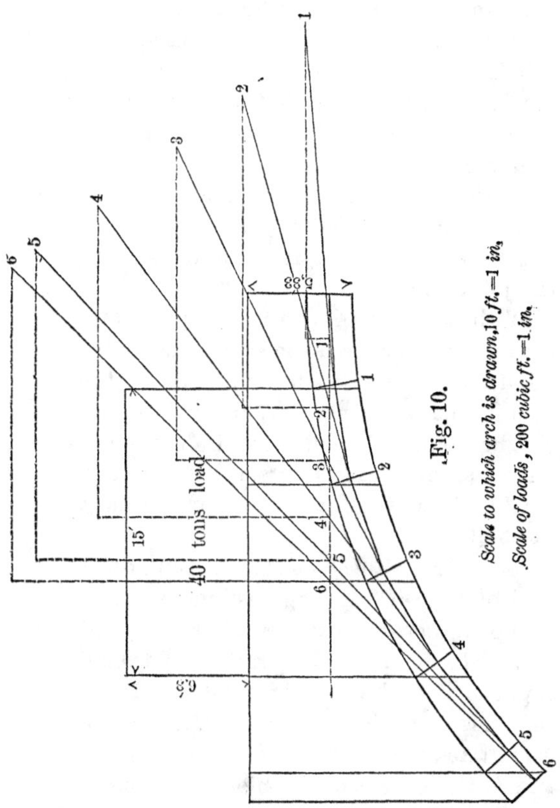

Fig. 10.

Scale to which arch is drawn, 10 ft.=1 in.

Scale of loads, 200 cubic ft.=1 in.

joint in question ; thus this error is not carried on. The ordinary method of constructing a line of pressures is to combine any resultant with the next weight following, regarded as concentrated at its centre of gravity.

By this construction any small error in draughting is carried on, whereas, by Dr. Scheffler's method, it is confined only to the joint where it occurs first.

With accurate instruments and care, using a sufficiently large scale, this method of Dr. Scheffler's should answer all the requirements of accuracy, and will generally be found the shortest in the end ; whereas, with many joints, it is difficult to locate this curve precisely by the ordinary method.

Second Example.—(Fig. 10.) Suppose a load of two 40-ton engines, one on each side of the crown, over divisions 2, 3, and 4, *i. e.*, 15 ft. along the rails. We shall suppose it to bear only on 6 ft. of the thickness of the viaduct. Calling the weight of a cubic foot of stone=.07 ton and *h*, the height of the block of stone 15 ft. long by 6 ft. wide that is required to weigh as much as one engine; we have

$$6 \times 15 \times h\ .07 = 40 \quad \therefore h = 6.3.$$

We now form the following table which refers to Fig. 10, which as the arch and load is symmetrical, represents, as before, only one-half the arch.

	w	v	s	c	m	S	M	C
1	5	5.4	27	2.5	67	27	67	2.5
2	5	12.4	62	7.5	465	89	532	6.
3	5	14.	70	12.5	869	159	1401	8.8
4	5	16.	80	17.5	1408	239	2809	11.8
5	5	13.2	66	22.5	1485	305	4294	14.1
6	1.75	14.5	25	25.9	658	330	4952	15.
			330		4952			

A line of pressures passing through the middle of the crown, the point on the springing joint, as before, will be found to be contained inside of the limiting curves, and is drawn as in Fig. 10, taking care to lay off the centres of gravity on the prolongation of Q. We find in this case $a = 25.6 - 15 = 10.6$, $P = 330$ $b = 10.7$.

$$\therefore Q = \frac{330 \times 10.6}{10.7} = 327 = \!\!\smile\!\!= 23 \text{ tons}.$$

If it is desired to draw the curve corresponding to the minimum of the thrust in the limits chosen, we resort to equations (2) and (3). As the nearest approach of the last line of pressures drawn to the outside limiting curve, is at joint 2; pass a curve of pressures now through the point of intersection of that outside limiting curve with the second joint and the previous point at the springing joint.

We find $P = 330$, $a = 10.6$, $e = 9.8$ and from table 2, column (S) $P_1 = 89$; from column (c) and the drawing $a_1 = 9.8 - 6 = 3.8$.

From (2)

$$\therefore Q = \frac{aP - a_1 P_1}{e} = \frac{3498 - 338}{9.8} = 322$$

From (3)

$$q = h - \frac{aP}{Q} = 11.93 - \frac{3498}{322} = 1.04$$

Laying off this latter distance, from the summit of the arch ring, downwards, we draw the curve as before. It is everywhere within the proper limits. It is not drawn in the figure as it passes very near the first curve.

If we suppose an engine of 13.3 tons weight to rest on division 3 on both sides of the crown, along 5 ft. of the length of the rails, we shall find by forming a table and constructing the line of pressures as before, that it passes slightly below the upper limit at the crown, and is everywhere contained in the middle third of the arch ring.

A curve of pressures for a uniform load of 1.5 tons per foot along the whole length of the bridge, will be found to follow very closely the curve drawn in the first example.

One or two more suppositions of isolated weights, symmetrically placed, were made, but in all cases it was found that a curve of pressures could easily be drawn in the inner third of the arch ring. The thrust is too small to fear crushing, and the directions of the thrust are inclined to the normals of the arch joints at angles much smaller than the angles of friction, hence sliding is not to be feared.

We conclude that thus far the arch has stability.

9.—It occurred to the writer that if the actual line of pressure in an arch composed of incompressible voussoirs, touched the contour curves, as shown in Art. 5, that it should hold very nearly in the case of experiments with light wooden arches, whose weight is not sufficient to produce much compressibility. It will be seen that this law is beautifully illustrated by these simple experiments.

The experiments by the writer were made with great care to endeavor to meet the requirements of an exact science.

Mr. Wm. Bland has published in Weale's series a book entitled, "Experimental Essays on the Principles of Construction in Arches, Piers, Buttresses, etc.," (1867), which contains experiments that we shall quote from. The preference will, however, be given to the writer's experiments, as we do not know *what care* Mr. Bland used in cutting out the voussoirs, in keeping the span invariable, piers vertical, and applying weights, etc.

To avoid mistake, the following nomenclature will be adopted:

Depth of a voussoir is the dimension in the direction of the radius of the intrados ⊥ to the axis of the arch.

Thickness of an arch or pier is the dimension ‖ to the axis of the arch.

Width of a pier is its horizontal dimension ⊥ to the axis of the arch.

Height is measured vertically.

The dimensions will all be given in inches.

A Gothic arch (Fig. 11) of 14 in. span, and 12.12 in. rise, was cut out of a poplar (tulip tree) plank, 3.65 in. thick, consisting of 8 voussoirs, each 3.65 thick, 2 deep, and 4.08 along their centre line from middle to middle of joint; each voussoir weighing .52 lb. Quite a number of voussoirs were cut out of the same layers of fibres and those selected that weighed exactly the same; the voussoir to be tried being hung to one end of a delicate balance beam, with a voussoir of the standard weight at the other end. The two voussoirs at the crown not being cut out of the same layers of fibres as the others, were shaved off about the middle of the extrados (not touching the joints) so as to weigh exactly 1 voussoir of the standard weight and their centres of gravity were found experimentally, and found to be at exactly similar points in both voussoirs, so that the entire arch was symmetrical as to the crown.

The centres of gravity of the other voussoirs are taken on the arc of a circle passing through the middle of the joints and for any voussoir equidistant from the joints bounding that voussoir. For voussoirs whose sides are little inclined, this is sufficiently near the truth, and by dividing the arch ring into a sufficient number of artificial voussoirs, the result may be made as accurate as we please. Still as no wood is homogeneous the results can only be regarded as approximate as compared with the hypothetical homogeneous arch ; still sufficiently near to establish the laws heretofore demonstrated.

When this arch was set up, the joints

apparently fitted perfectly, and on placing a drawing-board by the side of the arch and tracing off its contour curves, it was found to be a perfect Gothic whose arcs, composing the contour curves were correct arcs of circles described from the springing points opposite.

A number of rectangular wooden bricks of exactly 1 voussoir in weight, of various sizes, were also cut out, as well as half bricks, quarter bricks, etc., and some solid rectangular piers of various dimensions.

A voussoir is taken as the unit of weight.

In experiments where weights were placed upon the top of the arch, an assistant added brick after brick, carefully balancing the load at the top on either side by the fingers, until the arch reached its *balancing point; i. e.*, the point where it stood with the weight, but fell with a slight jarring.

The two bottom voussoirs were, when necessary, kept from sliding by two fastening tacks being driven into the board on which the arch rested, pressing against the arch .03 above the springing line, or so little that it may be disregarded. The board was carefully levelled at every experiment by a spirit level, and the span kept invariably at 14 in.

There was little or no vibration in the room.

First Experiment.—With 8.2 voussoirs on the summit of the arch it stood, though fell with 8.3 voussoirs on the summit; rotating on joints 2 on intradosal edge and at the summit; the arch being forced out at the haunches and falling at the crown. (See Fig. 11.)

The following table gives in its first column the number of joint from the crown; column *s*, the *elementary weights* (4.1 voussoir being the weight on the summit that goes to each abutment, the weight of each voussoir being taken as unity); column *m* gives the horizontal distance from the crown to the centre of gravity of each voussoir with its load, if any, which, in this case, is also the *moment* in reference to the vertical through the crown of each voussoir. Columns S, M, and C have been before explained.

.	s	m	S	M	C
	4.1	0.00	4.1	0.00	0 08
1	1.	1.70	5.1	1.70	.33
2	1.	4.68	6.1	6 38	1 04
3	1.	6.79	7.1	13.17	1.85
4	1.	7.88	8.1	21.05	2.6
	8.1	21.05			

Fig. 11.

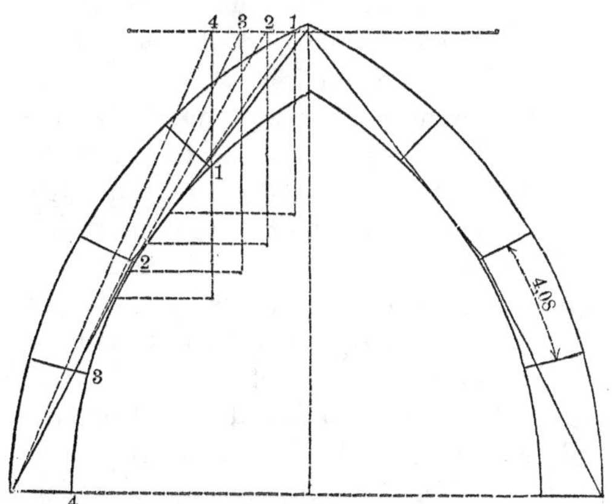

Try a line of pressures, passing 0.1 from the upper edge of crown joint (*i. e.* at the *summit*) and 0.1 from the extrados edge of the joint at the springing. From the drawing and table we find $a=6.3$, $b=14.27$, from which equation (1) gives us

$$Q=\frac{8.1\times 6.3}{14.27}=3.57$$

The line of pressures drawn with this value of Q and passing through the points indicated cuts joint 2 at 0.1 from its lower edge. From joint 0 to joint 2 the line of pressures corresponds to the minimum of the thrust ; from joint 2 to joint 4, to the maximum, for if the point of application at the crown is lowered to the point at joint 2, being moved from the edge, the same amount, the centre of pressure at joint 4 is moved to the left, outside its limiting position, which, as just seen, is in this arch 0.1 from the contour curves, for in *no other position* of the line of pressures than that first found, will it cut the joints of rupture 0,2 and 4, at the same distance from the contour curves, which, as the material of the voussoirs is nearly homogeneous, it is reasonable to conclude, should be the case. As there can be no greater nor less thrust, we conclude that the arch is on the limit of stability, as the experiment indicates.

0.1 is $\frac{1}{20}$ of the depth of joint.

Sliding would have occurred on joint 4, as the resultant on that joint made an angle of 24 deg. with the normal, but for the tacks before mentioned.

The diagrams for this and all the following experiments were drawn to a scale of one-third the natural size, except in the case of some of the pier experiments.

Second Experiment.—With the two voussoirs at the crown in one solid piece, the arch could not give by rotation, as the lower edge of crown joint could not open. With a sufficient pressure on the crown, there was sliding along joints 4, the coefficient of friction being small for these wooden blocks.

We evidently have here a sufficient reason for making the keystone in one solid piece.

Third Experiment.—On placing a knife edge against a notch .03 deep, cut into the bottom voussoir, 0.4 above the springing line, on each side, the arch balanced with 11.1 voussoirs on the summit. The line of pressures must now pass through the knife edges, and it will be found on constructing a diagram that it will pass about 0.1 from edges at joints 0 and 2, as before.

Fourth Experiment.—(Fig. 12.) The same arch stood, being very nearly on the balancing point, on *solid* piers 10. high, 1.9 wide, and 3.65 thick, each pier weighing 2.3 voussoirs, the intrados at the springing being at the inner edge of pier. The piers were made vertical by a spirit level, and their tops were upon the same level, in every experiment given.

In the following table the pier is included opposite joint 5 of the first column.

	S	c	m	S	M	C
1	1	1.7	1.70	1	1.70	1.7
2	1	4.68	4.68	2	6.38	3.19
3	1	6.79	6.79	3	13.17	4.39
4	1	7.88	7.88	4	21.05	5.26
5	2.3	7.95	18.28	6.3	39.33	6.24
	6.3		39.33			

To pass a curve of pressures 0.1 from the edges of joints 0 and 3, which will be found to correspond to the minimum of the thrust, we find from the above table and the drawing

$$Q = \frac{3 \times 2.2}{10.5} = .63$$

from which the curve of pressures in Fig. 12 is drawn, as before. This curve approaches the intrados nearest at joint 3, cuts joint 4 at .58 from the inner edge, and the base of the pier .2 from the outer edge or about $\frac{1}{10}$ the width of pier.

Fig. 12.

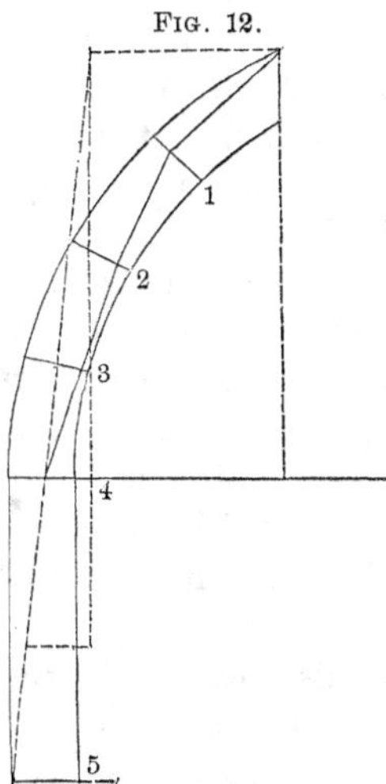

Fifth Experiment.—With piers 40.47 in. high, 3.65 wide, and 1.9 thick, weighing 10.1 voussoirs each, with the intrados of arch at springing on a line with inner edge of pier, the same arch balanced. The pier was built of a solid block 22 in. high, and 5 bricks placed on top, one above the other to make up the 40.47 in height.

A line of pressures drawn .1 from summit and .1 from intrados at joint 3, passes .5 from outer edge of pier, or about $\frac{1}{7}$ width of pier.

It will be found on constructing the diagrams for Mr. Bland's experiments, where the piers were built up of bricks, that in the case of low piers as in Figs. 51, 52, 53, 54, 55, 45 (*Exp.* No. 5), and 46 (*Exp.* 8), the line of pressures passes very near the outer edge of the base of the pier; but as the piers were increased in height, this line approaches more and more the centre of the base, being in the case of a pier 6 $\times$ 6 base and 72 in. high, nearer the centre of the base, than its outer edge.

It is probable that this is caused by the outer edge of every brick, when the line of pressures passes on that side of the centre, *compressing* a small quantity, as a great many irregular surfaces of contact must cause a greater compression than if the pier was solid. Again, the additional pressure on the lower bricks of a high pier is an evident cause for greater compression than with a low pier. A high pier of many bricks appears to *bend* in consequence of that compression of its many edges. It may be inferred from these facts that the greater the thrust in an arch the farther the line of pressures retreats within an arch; which we shall find to be so in the sequel.

Sixth Experiment.—The pier of *Exp.* 4 (Fig. 12) was moved outward (*from* the axis of the arch) so that when its inner edge was .1 from the springing, it stood with no weight on the summit; when it was .4 from edge, it stood with .5 vs., fell with .6 vs.; .5 from edge, balanced with .75 .vs.; .6 from edge balanced with .75 vs.; .7 from edge balanced with .37 vs.; 1.0 from edge balanced with .12 vs.

From which we infer that the centre of pressure at the springing joint is .5+5.1 (to allow for compression)=.65 from inner edge of joint for a weight of .75 vs. on the summit or apex of the arch. On constructing the table and diagram for this weight it will be found that theoretically the centre of pressure at the springing joint is .63 from the inner edge, which differing only .02 from the distance found by experiment must be regarded as a beautiful experimental illustration of the theory.

Seventh Experiment.—The same arch stood easily with .75 vs. on the summit, on solid piers, 22. high, 3.65 wide, and 1.9 thick each weighing 5.1 vs.; the arch fell with the addition of .12 vs. more.

On constructing this figure it will be found that the line of pressures, assumed 0.1 from edges of joints 0 and 3 as before, passes .63 from inner edge of springing joint (as was stated above) and cuts the base of pier .39 from its outer edge or about $\frac{1}{9}$ the width of pier.

Eighth Experiment.—On moving this pier back as in the 6th *Exp.*:

0.47 the arch balanced with 1.12 vs.
0.53 " " " " 1.25 "

.59	the	arch	balanced	with	1 25	vs.
.63	"	"	"	"	1.25	"
.7	"	"	"	"	1.12	"
1.	"	"	"	"	1.00	"

Taking .58 as the probable distance and adding .1, we get .68 as the probable distance back from the springing to the centre of pressure of joint 4. On constructing the line of pressures for a weight of 1.25 at the apex, passing 0.1 from the edge of joints 0 and 3 as before, it will be found that the centre of pressure on joint 4 is .7 from the edge, which is again a most striking coincidence, as it differs but .02 from the joint found experimentally. These experiments were made with great care, keeping the span exactly 14 inches, piers vertical, etc., etc.

Compare similar experiments by Mr. Bland (Figs. 56 and 57), where the same law is established approximately.

It is evident from an inspection of the arches in churches (for examples see drawings in the latter part of Mr. Bland's treatise) that constructors were well aware that a higher pier might be used when its inner edge was moved back a certain distance from the springing, which is equivalent to what we have established above.

Ninth Experiment.--With the pier used in *Exp.* 4, and the same arch, excepting that the two voussoirs at the crown were in one piece, the arch and pier just balanced as in *Exp.* 4. In fact, the arch and pier can easily rotate on the third joint and the outer edge of pier.

Tenth Experiment.—The same arch with piers 1.98 wide, 7.5 high and thickness of arch, each weighing 2 vs., stood easily when a cylindrical pin .03 in diameter was placed at the lower edge of crown joint. This joint bore at no other point, hence the line of pressures presses through the pin. Assuming it to pass .1 from the edge of joint 3, the construction will show that it cuts the springing joint .6 from inner edge and the base of pier .15 from its outer edge.

The *experiments* that we have just considered, very clearly indicate the fallacy of that theory which supposes that if a line of pressures passes outside the inner third of the arch ring, *that it must fall.* On the contrary, in every case of stability of the arches previously given, it is *impossible* to draw a line of pressures everywhere contained within the inner third of the arch ring. In fact, if such were attempted it would be found in every case that such a line of pressures would pass *outside* the base of the piers, or of the arch if used alone.

It is hardly probable, in most actual arches, that this line of pressures ever keeps within the inner third.

Theoretically, for the voussoir arch, there is no foundation for such a theory, and we confess to astonishment when we read in Prof. Rankine's "Engineering," Art. 280, "It is true that arches have stood, and still stand in which the centres of resistance of joints fall beyond the middle third of the depth of the arch ring; but the stability of such arches is either now precarious, or must have been precarious while the mortar was fresh."

As we have just asserted, in our experiments "the centres of resistance of joints" invariably fall outside the middle third, for certain joints, and if an experiment were made with a 50ft. arch it is not probable that at the joints of rupture, the centres of resistance would be found as far back from the edge as $\frac{1}{3}$ or even $\frac{1}{5}$ the depth of joint.

It may be well enough on account of the shocks to which bridges are subject to design an arch in which a line of pressures may be drawn within the inner third, but it is by no means necessarily true that the line of pressures can never pass this limit without the stability of the bridge being rendered precarious, though it would seem that this error has likewise been received in France (see "Traité de la Stabilité," etc., p. 220) by eminent mathematicians.

This subject will be referred to again in Art. 10. In all the experiments with arches the same voussoirs were used in the same positions each experiment.

Every experiment is given that was made, so that the reader may judge for himself how far the theory of Dr. Sheffler is established. No force diagram was drawn until after, and in some cases long after, the experiment was made; and no second trial was resorted to in any case.

All other writers but Dr. Scheffler, so far as the writer knows, have left the true line of pressures, in many cases at least, perfectly *indeterminate*, and it is Dr. Scheffler who has raised that indetermination by means of the principle of the least resistance and given us a theory which is upheld by experiment. Some authors actually assume the line of pressures to pass through the middle of the joint at the crown and springing.

It is evident how much more incorrect this is even than the fallacy of the "middle third."

Eleventh Experiment.—Fig. 13. With this same Gothic arch a segmental circular arch was now made of 24.24in. span, and 7in. rise; the voussoir being as before 2. deep and 3.65 thick.

With 7.6 vs. on the summit, this arch *balanced;* the weight being placed on a small stick resting on the summit. With a greater weight rotation occurred on joints 0, 2 and 4, the crown falling.

	s.	m.	S.	M.	C.
	3.8	0.00	3.8	0.00	.00
1	1.	2.03	4.8	2.03	.42
2	1.	5.90	5.8	7.93	1.37
3	1.	9.38	6.8	17.31	2.55
4	1.	12.11	7.8	29.42	3.77
	7.8	29.42			

FIG. 13.

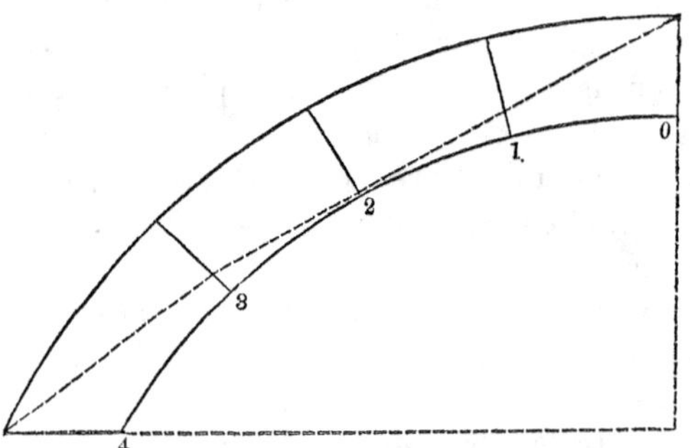

On trial it was found that the true line of pressures passes .15 from the edges at joints 0, 4 and 2; giving the characteristics of both a maximum and a minimum thrust. We find

$$Q = \frac{7.8 \times 10.45}{8.85} = 9.21 \; vs.$$

This horizontal thrust is greater than we have hitherto had, and probably accounts for the line of pressures retreating .05 further, in the arch ring, than we found for the Gothic arch. The construction is precisely similar to previous ones; the dotted line in Fig. 13 representing the line of pressures.

The ends of this arch required fastening tacks thrust into the board and pressing against voussoirs 4, .03 above the springing as in the first exp., with the Gothic, to prevent sliding. The thrust on joint 4 made an angle of 50° with the normal to that joint.

12*th Exp.*—With this arch resting on piers 3.63 wide, 5.8 high and 2. thick, each weighing 1.5 vs. the inner edge of pier being on a line with the springing, the arch balanced with .5 vs. on the summit.

We find, by constructing a line of pressures passing .15 from summit and the intrados at the third joint, that it cuts the base of pier .24 from its outer edge. Real arches have no mathematically plane joints, and therefore bear on the most elevated points.

This of itself may account for any *slight* discrepancies that we may meet with.

Some of Mr. Bland's experiments may now be tried, and they will be found to agree with the theory above ennunciated.

Thus in his first experiment, with a semi-circular arch of 24 in. span, the voussoirs being of wood, 2.5 deep and 4 thick, the arch being composed of 20 voussoirs; it stood with a weight equivalent to 2 vs. on the summit; falling with 2.5 vs.

The line of pressures passes very near the extrados at the crown and springing joints, and very near the intrados, half way between the crown and springing.

As in this experiment the weight probably bore on some extent of surface at the crown, and as the details of the method used to keep the bottom voussoirs from sliding are not given, and as besides the arch could not have been an exact semicircular, if the voussoirs were 2 in. in *length* (along their centre line from middle to middle of joint) the construction evidently shows only an approximation to the truth. The same remark applies to some other of the experiments.

The second exp. with a segmental arch is equally illustrative of the theory advanced, as also Exp. 5. In Figs. 51, 52 and 53 of arches on low piers, we likewise have a proof of the theory in question.

Fig. 51 of Mr. Bland's treatise represents the semi-circular arch just mentioned, *balancing* on piers 7 in. high, the base measuring 4x4. The line of pressure passes near the summit, near the intrados at about 30° above the springing and near the outer edge of pier.

The lines of pressure in the arches, Figs. 52 and 53, pass through, or very near the summit and springing, and the outer edge of the piers.

Figs. 55 and 57, of Mr. Bland's treatise, represent Roman arches on piers, which, together with Figs. 54 and 56 of Gothic arches on piers, and Figs. 45 and 46 of Roman arches with weights on them (exps.

with low piers), may be used to further illustrate Dr. Scheffler's theory.

In Chapter III of Mr. Bland's book are given numerous experiments of the effects of a horizontal force applied to the top of vertical piers built up of bricks of various heights and areas of base.

The reader will probably be surprised to find that, in the first 32 experiments given, if we regard the piers as *solid*, the actual horizontal forces exerted, to cause tumbling or rupture of some kind, was only three fourths, on an average, of the theoretical force required to cause *overturning* about an edge. The manner of rupture is not given by Mr. Bland, but it is evident especially from a consideration of his Fig. 26, that rupture was caused by *sliding* or sliding first and overturning afterwards.

In the few experiments of this kind by the writer, sliding usually occurred, even with brick piers; though overturning followed the sliding. Each brick seemed to have a different coefficient of friction, so that for these light piers, sliding often occurred some distance down from the top; though for blocks with the same angle of friction, the sliding ought to have occurred at the top.

It is true that in any case of overturning, the pier breaks along a diagonal and compresses at the edges, so as to cause leaning before overturning ; but this cannot alone account for the discrepancy mentioned above, perhaps.

13*th Exp*. To form some idea of the action of mortar of different degrees of hardness, pieces of cloth .07 thick when not pressed, and .04 thick when pressed between two flat surfaces by the hands were put between the joints of the Gothic arch, (Fig. 11), each piece weighing .015 voussoir.

The span was then altered until the joints were all close, when it was found to be 14.57, the rise to the apex being 14.55. On placing a drawing-board by the side of this arch and tracing its contour curves, they were found to be very nearly arcs of circles, though not with their centres at the springing points. To locate them; measure horizontally from the springing points .32 towards the middle of the span, and then vertically downwards 0.1 to the centres, from which the arch may be drawn.

This arch balanced with 4.6 vs. at apex.; fell with 4.65 vs. The limiting lines to the curve of pressures, was found to be distant $.3 = \frac{1}{7}$ depth of joint from the contour curves, at its nearest approach to them.

This arch spread outwards upon the application of the weights, joint 2 being the point of rupture at the haunches; hence it is evident that if there had been a solid spandrel, or in this case, simply the pressure of the hands, to resist this spreading, that the arch would not have fallen. The spandrel would have supplied horizontal forces in addition to the vertical ones due to its weight.

If the spandrel were not solidly built, at least up to joint 2, there would necessarily be derangement of the arch.

The curves of pressure were drawn in all the foregoing experiments, not taking into consideration the last mentioned derangement of the arch; which, in the last case especially, would have caused this curve to pass nearer the edges.

In fact, in most of the experiments, just before rotating, the edges alone seemed to be bearing. In the case of the simple Gothic, without cloth joints, when a sufficient weight was applied at the summit, the joint there, and joint 2, opened sensibly before the balancing weight was put on. The segmental arch flew out at the second joints, falling at the crown, only opening when near the balancing point.

Isolated weights applied at the summit, do not occur in practice, and it is hardly probable that a well-built viaduct, whose intrados is a segment of a circle, and of the proportions given in Fig. 9, with their joints only $\frac{1}{8}$ in. say, will spread appreciably after the mortar has well set; and this is necessarily a stronger form of arch than the semi-circular, elliptical, or hydrostatic, where the spandrel thrust is generally required to cause stability.

If the latter profiles are desired, let the

depth of the voussoirs be increased towards the abutment, so as to keep the line of pressures within the proper limits of the arch ring, when the constructor will be assured of stability.

It certainly seems singular, that engineers should ever *recommend* an arch like the hydrostatic, which necessarily requires a very effective spandrel thrust to keep the arch from tumbling down.

The spandrels must in such cases be built with the same care used with the arch stones; thus increasing the *expense*, while really losing in *strength*.

14*th Exp*. In the joints of the same Gothic arch, pieces of soft woolen cloth .15 thick when not pressed, and .1 when pressed hard between two bricks by the hands, were next inserted, each piece of cloth weighing .027 voussoir. The span, when the joints were close, was found to be 15 in.; rise to apex, 14.63. The centres for describing the contour curves were 1.07 in. from the springing points measured horizontally towards the middle of span.

This arch balanced with 2.3 vs. on the apex.

Assuming this arch to preserve its figure, the curve of pressures passes about one fourth the depth of joint from the edges at its nearest approach to them.

This experiment gives us some idea of the effect of thick plastic mortar joints or of uncentreing an arch with fresh mortar joints.

15*th Exp.* A Gothic arch of about half the dimensions of the first given in *Exp.* 1 was cut out; really, before the arch we have just been considering.

It was not found to be symmetrical as to weight, one half weighing $\frac{1}{32}$ of the whole arch more then the other half. Still as arches in practice are unsymmetrical as to weight at least; it will be interesting to know, that assuming this arch to be symmetrical the curve of pressures passes .075 from the edges at the joints of rupture, more especially with weights at the apex.

All the preceding experiments were repeated with this arch and the same laws approximately established.

In the experiment with the cloth joints, the cloth was .05 thick not pressed; .04 when pressed hard by the hand. The curve of pressures was found to pass .1 from the edges at the joints of rupture, with a weight on the apex, and nearly so in the pier experiment with no weight on the apex.

16*th Exp.* Mr. Bland gives, (p 21,) an example of a Gothic arch of 24 in. span, voussoirs 2.5 deep, which fell of its own weight; though it was partly built of flat bricks, which accounts for its falling, for on making an arch of the above proportions it not only stood easily, but all the above principles were approximately established by it. The arch was not perfectly symmetrical as to weight, and was composed of 16 voussoirs; span 10.7 in.

The line of pressures passed within .075 of the edges at the joints of rupture.

The arch given by Mr. Bland, was probably not a true Gothic, or the joints did not fit along their whole extent; a sufficient hint to the constructor to exercise every care in these particulars in building.

It is to be regretted that in the experiments given by Mr. Bland, where backing was used, that he does not state its thickness, except in the case of some experiments with models of bridges.

In the model of the Rochester bridge, Fig. 81, where the backing was carried up on a level with the summit of the arch ring, the line of pressures will be found by the method of Art. 8 to pass very near the edges at the summit, the springing and the outer edge of pier.

This experiment especially shows the error of passing a curve of pressures through the middle of the joints at the crown and springing, or within the middle third of the arch.

The bridge would have tumbled on either supposition. This bridge was 100 ft. span, and 15 ft. rise; the model having a span of 15 in. and a rise of 3.75 inches.

A series of extensive experiments on large arches, of stone or even wood, somewhat after the manner of these, is much to be desired as they would show us practically the effect of the compressibility of the materials upon the line of pressures.

Thus suppose stone or even wood arches of 10, 20, 30, 40, 50 and 100 feet spans to be cut out, and the balancing weights, at the crown, found. The distance that the line of pressures retreats from the edges follows, and we thus have practical data to work from, in designing similar arches; besides the law of that compressibility may be approximately found.

An example will now be given of a combination of the method used by Dr. Scheffler and that by the writer. Calling r, in Fig. 14, the radius of the extrados, r_1, that of the intrados and n the proportion of the circumference included by the voussoir, we have its content $= \frac{\pi (r^2 - r_1{}^2)}{n}$ for a thickness of 1. Now this is equal to $\left[\text{the depth, } (r - r_1) \times \text{the } \textit{middle length} \left(\frac{2 \pi (r + r_1)}{n \times 2} \right) \right] = \frac{\pi (r_2 - r_1{}^2)}{n}$; hence measure the middle length and depth on a drawing, their product will give the required volume.

We now form the following table for Fig. 14, where the dimensions of the voussoir are given just below the dimensions of the corresponding surcharge. This manner of considering the voussoirs and surcharge separately is continued until in columns S and M, the quantities referring to the same joint are combined by the continued addition of the quantities in columns S and M separately.

If the voussoirs are taken the same size, there is really no necessity of entering their dimensions; simply giving their common area in columns.

This manner of computing the surfaces (S) and their lever arms (C) is particularly applicable in the case of tunnel arches, which often have quite a depth of voussoir; as for example the Thames Tunnel, whose span is 14 feet, the depth of the arch ring being 3 feet.

This method gives all the accuracy that is necessary in practice; expecially as arches are never symmetrical as to weight, and besides their spreading, if any, at the haunches requires an allowance to be made.

FIG. 14.

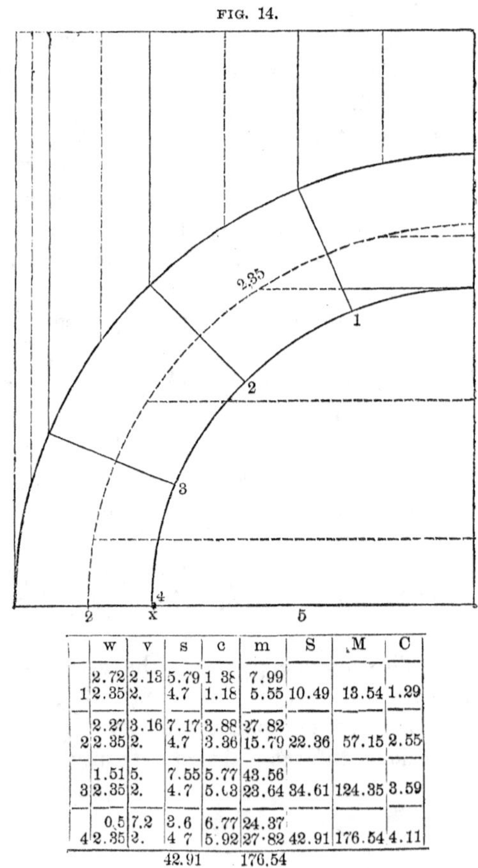

	w	v	s	c	m	S	M	C
1	2.72 2.35	2.13 2.	5.79 4.7	1.38 1.18	7.99 5.55	10.49	13.54	1.29
2	2.27 2.35	3.16 2.	7.17 4.7	3.88 3.36	27.82 15.79	22.36	57.15	2.55
3	1.51 2.35	5. 2.	7.55 4.7	5.77 5.03	43.56 23.64	34.61	124.35	3.59
4	0.5 2.35	7.2 2.	3.6 4.7	6.77 5.92	24.37 27·82	42.91	176.54	4.11
			42.91		176.54			

In experiments with arches with a backing, this method is especially applicable, particularly with full centre arches.

The decimals in the foregoing table are not carried out as far as they should be in practice.

10.—The manner in which rotation occurs in an arch will be made clear from a consideration of Figs. 6 and 15. Suppose the resultant R to pass outside the arch ring at any point, and that it is not opposed by any resistance there; next conceive two equal opposed forces, || to R, to be applied at some point p (Fig. 15) of the joint. This evidently does not disturb the equilibrium.

Fig. 15.

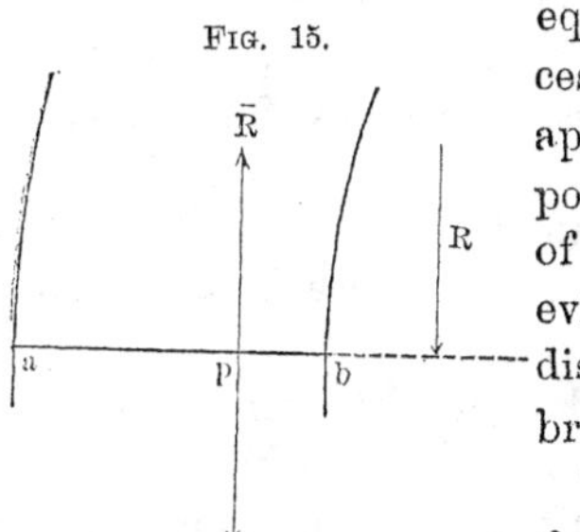

We see, that there is a couple $R\bar{R}$ formed together with a force equal and || to R acting in the direction of R at p; which last is resisted by the compressive reaction at the joint. The couple R, $\bar{R}$

can only be resisted by a couple; hence if there are tensile forces towards a, to be combined with the compressive reactions, a *resisting* couple may be formed of sufficient moment to maintain the equilibrium, and this is what usually happens in a solid arch of cast iron or concrete, etc.; but it is evident that if the joint can supply no tensile resistance, as in the case of a plane joint without mortar, or with mortar whose cohesive strength is null, then rotation must occur, as there is an unbalanced couple to produce it.

In fact (see Fig. 6) if the resultant R in any compressible arch, without tensile resistance at the joints, approaches nearer the edge than *its limiting* position, an unresisted couple is at once formed and overturns the arch.

To consider the voussoir arch, whose joints can supply no tensile resistances, further, let us suppose first, the resultant R, (Fig. 6) to be in the centre of the joint; the forces f- - -, f'- - - may for a small joint be regarded as uniformly distributed. Suppose now the resultant R to move towards the edge *b*, slightly; there is still only *compression* on the joint, though its distribution is according to some unknown law. There is no couple formed until R has passed its limiting position, as is clearly shown by the preceding experiments; otherwise rotation would have occurred, which however did not happen.

In fact in moving the position of the resultant (Fig. 6) from the centre of the joint towards *b*, the stress becomes greater at *b* than at *a*; and some line $s\,s'$ will limit the values of the elementary forces f - - - - f' - - - -, representing them by arrows as in the figure.

We cannot, however, locate the line $s\,s'$ with our present knowledge, except in certain positions of R for solid arches, where actual tensile forces are brought into play; the usual theory for that case being as follows: Suppose the resultant R to be treated as in Fig. 15, the two equal opposed forces being supposed applied at the neutral axis or centre of gravity of the cross section of the beam.

The couple R $\overline{\text{R}}$ is resisted by the tensile and compressive resistances, acting respectively on either side of the neutral axis, as in the case of ordinary flexure of a beam. The remaining force, acting ∥ and in the direction of R, at the neutral axis, being decomposed into its elements, adds to some of the forces brought into play by the couple R $\bar{R}$ and subtracts from others.

FIG. 16.

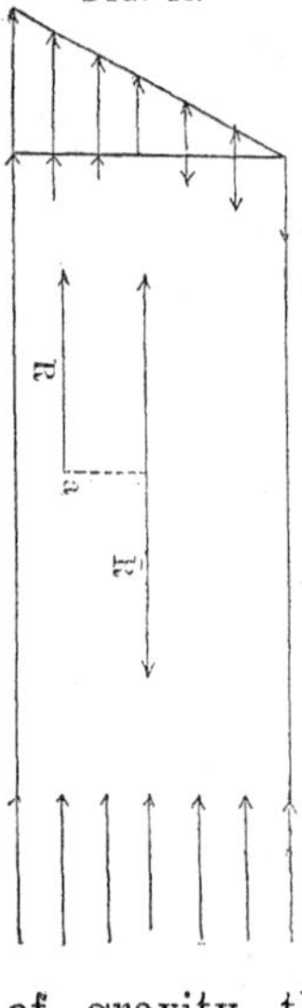

Let us suppose the resultant R to approach the centre of gravity of the cross section; when it reaches a point a, which is $\frac{1}{6}$ the depth of beam from the centre of gravity, for a rectangular cross section, varying for other forms, there are no real tensile forces exerted at the joint (Fig. 16); and as a approaches nearer the centre of gravity the determination of the elementary forces at any point becomes uncertain.

In the solid arch, when R is farther from the centre of gravity than the point a, tensile forces are exerted about the farther edge, which, together with the compressive forces, form a couple, which transports the resultant R nearer the centre of gravity of the cross section.

In the voussoir arch, whose joints oppose no tensile resistance, however, there is no resisting couple to effect this transfer of the resultant, and it is absurd to suppose the two equal opposed forces at the neutral axis, in which case the arch cannot be supposed to resist the couple inevitably formed; with the same propriety might the two opposed forces be supposed, in the first instance, on the farther side of the arch ring; and yet certain authors seem to think that the line of pressures cannot pass outside the middle third of the arch ring without a couple being formed, and rupture ensuing, whereas our experiments have clearly proved that for the arches used this line of pressures passed on an average only $\frac{1}{18}$ the depth of joint from the edge at the joints of rupture, without rupture ensuing.

As the joints opened in many of the exps. before rotation occurred, it is evident that if the joint had been capable of offering tensile resistance, that it would have come into play, and prevented the opening; thus carrying the resultant nearer the centre and causing a more

Fig. 17.

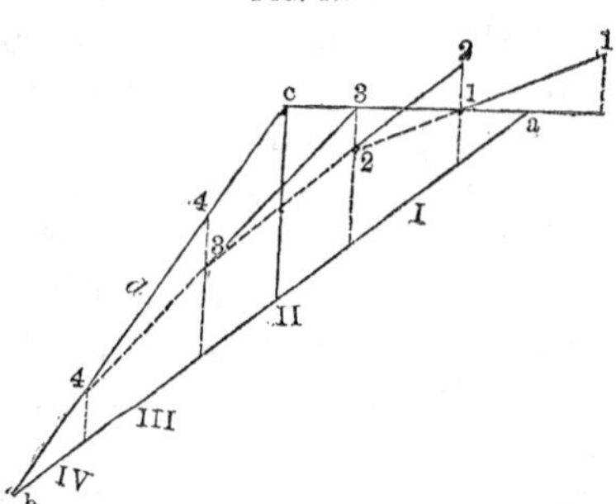

equal distribution of the resistance on the joint, than where the arch opposed no tensile resistance. Hence the utility of concrete arches, which can oppose such resistances, as also of solid metal and timber arches.

A good illustration of the agreement between algebraical formulæ and graphic construction, may be had from a consideration of two inclined rafters leaning against each other, one of which (supposed of very small cross-section) is represented by *ab* in Fig. 17.

Reasoning as in Art. 2, we see that the thrust at the crown is horizontal ; and if $\overline{c\,\text{II}}$ = weight of beam drawn through its centre of gravity, $\frac{1}{2}\,c\,a$ is the horizontal thrust.

Divide the length of the beam into any number of equal parts, four in the figure; combine as by the ordinary method, the horizontal thrust, at *a*, with the weight of the first division of the rafter, acting through its centre of gravity. Combine this resultant with the weight of the next division and so on. The last resultant $\overline{44}$ should pass through *b* and equal the thrust there, $\overline{cd}$ and act in the same direction. The other method of construction adopted in this article may likewise be used, particularly for many divisions of the rafter. The bending moment on joint I is the length $\overline{11}$, multiplied by a perpendicular, from the neutral axis at joint I, to its direction; that on joint II is $\overline{22} \times$ perpendicular from II, to its direction and so on for the others.

Fig. 18.

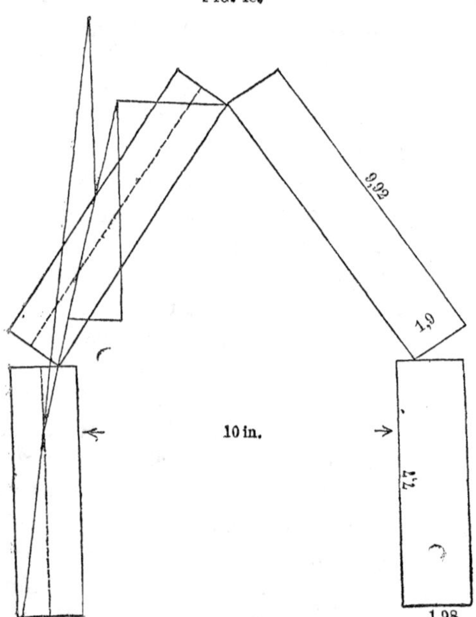

Now if by the usual formulæ for an inclined beam, we calculate these moments, they will be found to exactly correspond to those found above, mostly by graphic construction. The *curve of equilibrium* $\overline{a1234b}$, as the curve of pressures is sometimes called, is, for a beam of uniform weight per unit of length, a parabola, whose vertex is at a, as is well known.

The component of any resultant, perpendicular to the beam, is the shearing force on the joint to which the resultant corresponds; the parallel components give the direct compressive force on the beam.

By algebraical formulæ, we know that the bending moment at I is equal to that at III, that at a and b, being zero; also the shearing force at a equals that at b, at I, that at III; all of which we find by this partly graphic method.

Figure 18 represents two rafters 9.92 in length, 1.9 width (dimension in plane of paper) and 3.60 thick, leaning against each other at the top and against piers 7.7 high, 1.98 wide and 3.6 thick at their bottom edge, which is moved back 0.6 from the edge of the pier. The horizontal distance between the vertical piers is 10 in., so that the feet of the rafters are 11.2 apart. Each rafter weighed 2.3 vs.; each pier 2. vs. The rafters and piers just balanced in this position.

Reasoning as in Art. 2, we see that the thrust at the upper edges of contact of the rafters is horizontal; hence draw a vertical line through the centre of gravity of the rafter equal to its weight; the resultant on the lower edge of the rafter passes through this edge, which combined with the weight of the pier acting through its centre of gravity, gives the resultant thrust on the base of the pier. In this case it strikes twenty-two hundredths(.22) from its outer edge.

There is to be found in many standard works an erroneous theory of this case, which supposes half the weight of the two rafters to be suspended at the upper points of contact. If the reader will decompose this weight into its two components acting along the rafters, and then combine a component with the weight of the pier, he will find that the final resultant.ᵗ will pass .83 outside the base of the pier, and yet it stood well. The same thing may be seen on investigating Mr. Bland's exps. on rafters, p. 70. Until such palpable errors as we have noted along, are expunged from text books, the young engineer cannot be said to have a safe guide in the theory of his profession; and ye old practical man will ever smile at the attempts to reconcile theory with practice.

The next Fig. (19.), represents a rafter and pier of the preceding experiment; the rafter leaning against a vertical rough plastered wall by its edge, the lower edge resting on the pier 1.03 back from its inner edge. This was the balancing position. The construction is as before explained in Art. 1, for Fig. 1.

After several trials, assuming as we found in the preceding experiment that the resultant strikes .22 from the outer edge of the base of pier, it was found that the direction of the thrust against the wall was inclined about 35° to the horizontal, which is about what we should imagine the angle of friction of the edge on the wall was. This proves the first proposition in Art. 1. Even if the thrust at the upper edge be assumed horizontal, it will be found that the final resultant passes outside the base of pier; hence, such an assumption is false. The construction (Fig. 19.) by extension, will also show that .32 v. of the rafter is sustained by the wall, 1.98 v. being supported by the pier; *i. e.* about one seventh of the weight of the rafter is upheld by the friction of the plastered wall.

On leaning a half arch against a wall, it was found to balance on higher piers than when the other half was placed against it.

11. It would be beyond the scope of this article, to follow Dr. Scheffler in the discussion of horizontal, as well as vertical forces applied to the arch, which however presents no difficulty. As all inclined forces can be resolved into vertical and horizontal components, it follows that his discussion applies to any form of arch, solicited by forces inclined in any

direction. A profile may be designed, by simply assuming first some form of arch deemed the best; then drawing its curve

Fig. 19.

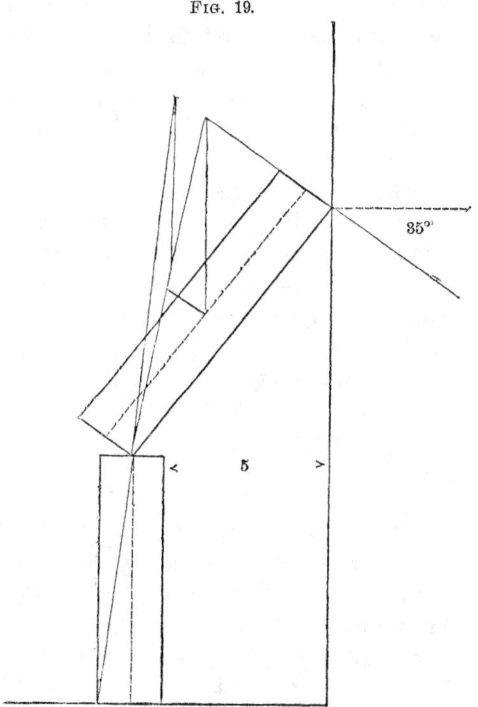

of pressures for the load passing through the middle of the joints at the crown and springing, and taking this curve as the centre line of the desired arch ring, when it will generally be found that the curve of pressures for this last arch will remain everywhere within the proper limits; a second trial being rarely, if ever needed, in practice.

Thus we find that the strongest form of arch, with a very high surcharge of masonry is the parabola. Dr. Scheffler found by a construction of this kind that the ellipse was the best form for an underground tunnel.

The simplicity and accuracy of Dr. Scheffler's method must commend it to practical engineers.

UNSYMMETRICAL ARCHES.

12. Dr. Scheffler demonstrates in this case, for incompressible voussoirs, what curve of pressures corresponds to the minimum of the thrust, and is therefore the true one. It would lead us too far here to enter into this discussion. The

most usual case, being probably the only one met with in practice, furnishes this characteristic for the minimum thrust; *that it has two points of contact with the intrados and an intermediate point common with the extrados*, which is identical with what we have before found for symmetrical arches. This case includes that, where the points of meeting the intrados are at the springing.

There is a joint, EF (Fig. 20) generally near the crown at which the thrust is horizontal. Where the arch is only solicited by vertical forces, by compounding them with this thrust, as before, we find the resultants on every joint, and it is evident in this case that the horizontal thrust is the same all through the arch.

It is more convenient however, to find the inclined thrust at the crown and combine the partial weights with it, to find the resultant on each joint.

Problem : To find this inclined thrust and its point of application :

Let I, L, K be three points through

which we wish to pass a curve of pressures (Fig. 20) $\overline{ACB}$ a horizontal line drawn through the highest point of the extrados, and let there be:

Q the horizontal thrust, *i. e.* the horizontal component of any one whatsoever of the pressures acting through I, L, K.;

P the vertical component of the pressure S at the crown joint, which will be considered positive, if it is directed upwards, as regards pressure from the right part upon the left; in fact P may be regarded as a supporting force, when to the right of the joint E F, for if the arch only extended to C, P would be the weight that would be supported or resisted there; and so for any point of the arch to the right of E F.

Let q, be the vertical distance of the point of application of S below the horizontal $\overline{ACB}$; g_1, h_1; g_2, h_2; g_3, h_3, the horizontal and vertical co-ordinates of I, K and L as to the point C as the origin;

P^{I}, P^{II}, P^{III}, the vertical components of the pressures acting through I, K and L;

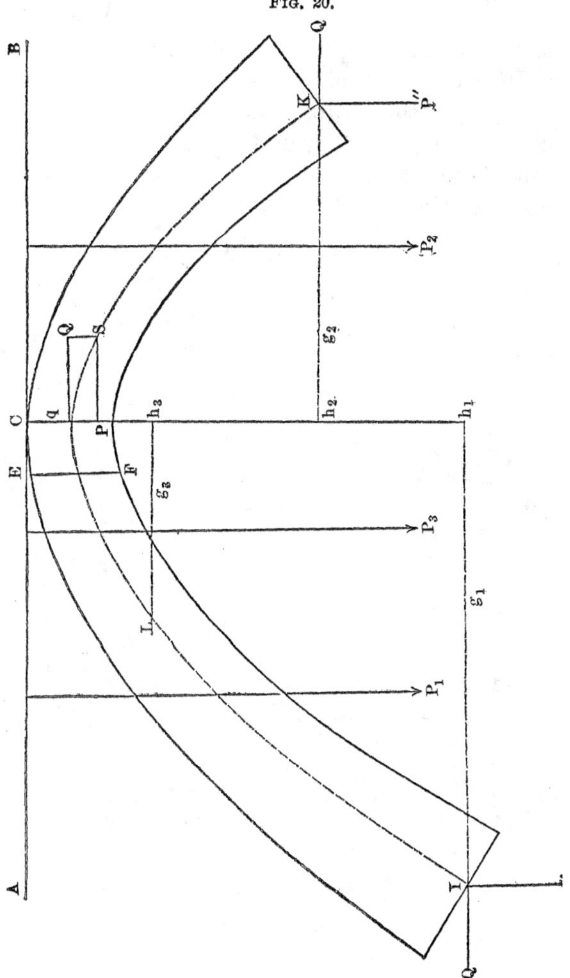

FIG. 20.

P_1, P_2, P_3, the weights of the segments C I, CK, CL, with their loads;

p_1, p_2, p_3, the horizontal distances of the centres of gravity of these segments from the point C.

To abbreviate, let us put:

$g_1 - p_1 = a_1$	$g_2 - p_2 = a_2$	$g_3 - p_3 = a_3$
$h_1 - q = b_1$	$h_2 - q = b_2$	$h_3 - q = b_3$
$g_2 x g_3 = d_1$	$g_1 - g_3 = d_2$	$g_1 x g_2 = d_3$
$h_1 - h_3 = e_1$	$h_1 - h_3 = e_2$	$h_1 - h_2 = e_3$

We have:

$$P^1 + P = P_1 \quad - - - - - - - - - - \quad (1)$$
$$P^{11} - P = P_2 \quad - - - - - - - - - \quad (2)$$
$$a_1 P_1 - g_1 P = b_1 Q \quad - - - - - - - - \quad (3)$$
$$a_2 P_2 \times g_2 P = b_2 Q \quad - - - - - - - \quad (4)$$
$$a_3 P_3 - g_3 P = b_3 Q \quad - - - - - - \quad (5)$$

If the third given point L of the curve of pressures is upon the joint at the crown C, the value of q is known, and we have: $g_3 = o$, $h_3 = q$, $P_3 = O$. From eqs. (3) and (4) we find

$$P = \frac{a^1 b_2 P_1 - a_2 b_1 P_2}{g_1 b_2 + b_1 g_2} = \frac{a_1 e_1 P_1 - a_2 e_2 P_2}{e_2 d_3 - e_3 d_2} \quad ..(6)$$

$$Q = \frac{a_1 P_1 - g_1 P}{b_1} = \frac{a_1 d_1 P_1 + a_2 d_2 P_2}{e_2 d_3 - e_3 d_2} \quad \ldots\ldots(7)$$

If L is not upon the joint at the summit, we find*

$$P = \frac{a_1 e_1 P_1 - a_2 e_2 P_2 + a_3 e_3 P_3}{e_2 d_3 - e_3 d_2} \quad \ldots(8)$$

$$Q = \frac{a_1 d_1 P_1 + a_2 d_2 P_2 - a_3 d_3 P_3}{e_2 d_3 - e_3 d_2} \quad \ldots(9)$$

$$q = h_1 - \frac{a_1 P_1 - g_1 P}{Q} \quad \ldots\ldots(10)$$

Example 1. Fig. 21 represents the same viaduct, before considered in Art. 8, with a load of 40 tons on 15 feet of length over divisions 2, 3 and 4, on one side of the arch only. Table 1 (Art. 8) refers to the right half of the arch : table 2 of the same article to the left side.

---

* Add (4) and (3) and call the sum eq. (13); also subtract (5) from (3). Place the values of Q equal to each other in this last eq. and eq. (13); reducing, bearing in mind that $d_3 - d_2 = d_3$, $e_2 - e_3 = e_1$, &c., we find P as in eq. (8). Substitute this value of P just found in eq. (11) and deduce Q, which gives eq. (9). Eqs. (6) and (7) are only particular cases of eqs. (8), (9) and (10) when $P_3 = O$.

Let us pass a curve of pressures through the middle of the crown and through a point, on each springing joint, $\frac{1}{3}$ depth joint above its lower edge.

We find from the drawing and tables

$g_1 = g_2 = 25.6, \quad b_1 = b_2 = 10.75$
$P_1 = 330, \quad p_1 = 15, \quad a_1 = 10.6$
$P_2 = 236, \quad p_2 = 16, \quad a_2 = 9.6$

From (6):

$$P = \frac{a_1 b_2 P_1 - a_2 b_1 P_2}{g_1 b_2 + b_1 g_2} = 24 \text{ cubic ft. of stone};$$

from (7):

$$Q = \frac{a_1 P_1 - g_1 P}{b_1} = 268 \text{ cubic ft. of stone};$$

From M, the middle of the crown joint, lay off downwards $\overline{MN} = P$, also $\overline{NH} = Q$ on the horizontal through N; $\overline{MH}$ will then represent the resultant on the crown joint in direction position and magnitude; and by combining it with the weight of each artificial voussoir and load, on each side of the crown, each acting through its centre of gravity, we evidently obtain the resultants on the various joints in direction, position and magnitude, and therefore can trace the curve of pressures. For example, to find the resultant on the third joint on the left side of the arch: draw a horizontal line through M and lay off on it the distance of the centre of gravity of the three first divisions, from M, which by Table 2 (Art. 8), column C, is found to be 8.8.

Draw a vertical through this point and from its point of intersection with $\overline{MH}$, lay off upwards the weight 159 (column S) of the three divisions in question.

From the upper extremity of this last line draw a line ‖ and equal to $\overline{MH}$; completing the parallelogram of forces as per figure, the point where the resultant cuts joint 3 is the centre of pressure of that joint, and the resultant is given in magnitude, position and direction by the diagonal.

The construction for the other joints is the same.

The nearest approach of the curve of pressures to the extrados is on joint 2, of the left side of the arch, where it is only three tenths (.3) of a foot (on a large scale drawing it was found to be .35) from the edge. The nearest approach to the intrados is at joints 3, 4 and 5 on the right, being only about .7 to .75 from the edges at those joints. Hence if we desire the curve of pressures, with this load, to remain in the middle third of the present arch ring, we must increase its depth about .6 ft. making the arch stones 3.1 ft. in depth.

It will be interesting to compare some empirical formulæ with this result. Dr. Rankine gives * for the "depth of keystone for a single arch.

in feet $= \sqrt{(\cdot 12 \times \text{radius at crown})}$"
$= \sqrt{.12 \times 36.25} = 2.1.$

Depth of keystone for an arch of a series, in feet $= \sqrt{(.17 \times \text{radius at crown}} = 2.5.$

Mr. J. C. Trautwine gives † for that span and rise 2.16 as the proper depth of keystone.

By interpolation from Dr. Scheffler's tables ‡ we find that he recommends in this case 3.5 ft. depth of keystone.

* "Civil Engineering," Art 290.
† "Engineer's Pocket-book," p. 345.
‡ "Traite de la Stabilité," pp. 257, 277.

It must be remembered that when a locomotive passes rapidly over a bridge, that the principle of the least resistance can only apply approximately, as *it takes time* for molecular resistances to come into play; besides the shocks and concussions are the more damaging the smaller the bridge, hence while there is probably stability of the arch (Fig. 21) for a quiescent load of a 40-ton engine, it is not so certain for a moving load of that weight.

As the spandrels are not capable of exerting much resistance above joint 2, it seems that it would be advisable to increase the depth of keystone to three feet.

In fact while engineers have continued to increase the size of pieces in wood and iron bridges, as heavier engines were used, in some cases to double the size once used, yet they recommend for stone bridges the same depth of keystone that has been found to answer for road bridges built many years ago. We are indebted to Dr. Scheffler, now, for the means of completely investigating symmetrical or unsymmetrical arches, with any kind of loads, vertical or

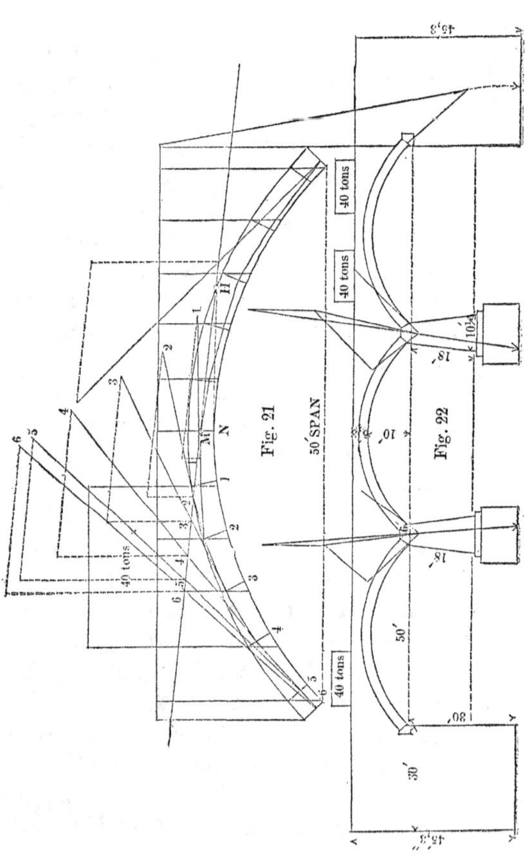

Fig. 21

Fig. 22

inclined, upon the hypothesis of incompressible voussoirs; besides we may be said at last to have got upon the right track of investigation as deduced from the principle of the least resistance; hence we should be no longer confined to purely empirical formulæ.

When we shall know the laws of elasticity, the theory may be regarded as complete for a statical load.

It looks probable, however, from a consideration of the experiments with the wooden arches, as well as cases in practice, that the theory for incompressible materials is not modified greatly; and it is more likely that severe shocks may have a greater influence in modifying that law, than the compressibility of the materials used. A considerable margin should always be left for these influences.

Example 2. A load of 13.3 tons was assumed on division, 3 on one side, and it was found that a curve of pressures could be drawn, for this eccentric load, within the inner third of the arch ring.

If the backing is raised higher, thus

making the bridge weigh more, a rolling load will have less effect upon it ; hence a less depth of keystone may be used. Other things the same, it is a simple question of economy, considering the approaches, whether to increase the height of surcharge above the arch ring, or the depth of the arch stones. The bridge considered could have the backing raised a foot higher with advantage.

Fig. 22 shows the effect of rolling loads in different positions, on the piers ; the middle bay not being loaded but with its own weight, the end spans as per figure. The resultants at the springing joints we have before determined ; combining the two on any pier with the weight of pier, according to the usual rule for three forces not intersecting in one point, we obtain the final resultants on the base of the piers. It is seen in Fig. 22, that in both cases, the resultant falls inside the base a sufficient quantity for a rock foundation, though probably not for a soft one.

It is seen from the figure that the 40 tons on both sides produce a more hurtful effect on the pier than a 40 ton load on one side only.

By combining the weight of abutment with the thrust on it, we find that the centre of pressure on the foundation course is sufficiently within the limits for most cases in practice.

The dotted line in the abutment gives the centres of pressure of all the forces acting on each joint for the joints in question. For example, to find where this centre of pressure is on the springing line, produced, we combine the inclined resultant on the arch joint at the springing with the weight of the abutment above the springing line, acting through its centre of gravity. This resultant makes an angle with the vertical of only 23°, hence sliding on the springing course is not to be feared, if the abutment is solidly built. This centre of pressure must not be confounded with the points of greatest intensity of stress which includes the springing, but cannot be farther traced in the abutment composed of a number of stones.

We have considered the stability of this

common form of viaduct under every point of view necessary in practice, and in the same manner can other forms of arch be investigated.

Fig. 23.

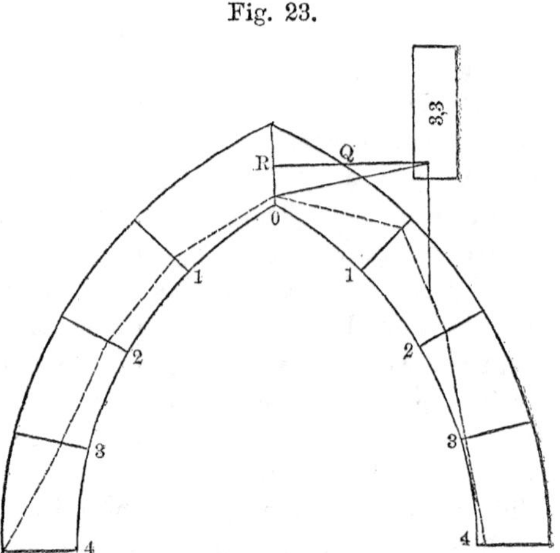

If in any arch the first trial curve passes outside the proper limits, mark the joint limits opposite the points of greatest departure and pass a curve through three points thus found by the use of eqs. (8), (9) and

(10). If the arch has stability at all, it will generally be found that this last curve drawn will remain in the proper limits; otherwise repeat the operation.

It would lead us too far to consider inclined forces, which are fully discussed by Dr. Scheffler and offer but little difficulty.

First Experiment. The Gothic arch given by Fig. 11 will now be considered with an unsymmetrical load. A stout needle was thrust into the second voussoir from the crown on the right side, in the direction of a vertical through its centre of gravity, as represented in Fig. 23. With a weight of 3.3 vs. on the top of the needle, the arch balanced; opening at summit and lower edge of joint 1 on the right. The voussoir to which the weight was added would have slid if pins had not been thrust into the edges of its joints, thus supplying a force analogous to friction, though not interfering at all with rotation.

We now form the following tables; the first being condensed from the one referring to Exp. 3, in Art. 9:

LEFT SIDE.

	S	C
1	1	1.70
2	2	3.19
3	3	4.39
4	4	5.26

RIGHT SIDE.

	s	C	M	S	M	
1	1.	1.7	1.70	1.	1.70	1.70
2	4.3	4.68	20.12	5 3	21.82	4.12
3	1.	6.79	6.79	6.3	28.61	4.54
4	1	7.88	7.88	7.3	36.49	5.
	7.3		36.49			

As the crown joint bore near the lower edge and the first joint on the right near its upper edge; try a curve of pressures passing .1 from those edges and .1 from the extrados on joint 4 on the left.

We find

$$g_1 = 8.9 \qquad g_2 = 3.9$$
$$a_1 = 3.64 \qquad a_2 = 2.2$$
$$b_1 = 12.2 \qquad b_2 = 0.65$$
$$P_1 = 4. \qquad P_2 = 1.0$$

By Eqs. (6) and (7) we find

$$P = \frac{3.64 \times .65 \times 4 - 2.2 \times 12.2}{8.9 \times .65 + 12.2 \times 3.9} = - .326$$

$$Q = \frac{3.64 \times 4 + 8.9 \times .326}{12.2} = 1.43$$

P. is here minus, hence we lay it off upwards, then measuring Q to the right we get the resultant S at the crown from which the line of pressures may be drawn as in Example 1 of this article.

The line of pressures drawn with these values of P and Q passes .36 from the lower edge of joint 3 on the right. It should pass the same distance from the edges at joint 4 on the left, the crown and joints 1 and 3 on the right, to correspond to the maximum and the minimum of the thrust, hence this curve just found is not the true one.

In two more trials, it was found that the true line of pressures passed about .18 from the edges just mentioned, as drawn in Fig. 23.

Although the characteristics of the minimum and the maximum of the thrust are not demonstrated, the reader will perceive that there should be stability in this case as the line of pressures is inside the proper limits. The lower edge of the crown joint

FIG. 24.

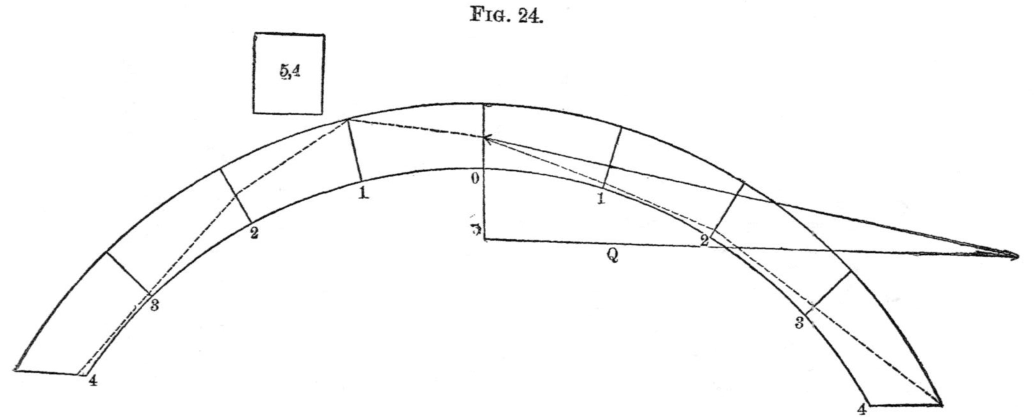

was imperfect, being the only imperfect edge in the arch, and this may account for the line of pressures re treating farther in the arch than for a load on the summit as before considered.

The thrust on joint 1, on the right, was inclined at an angle of 15° to the normal to that joint, which accounts for the sliding, as the joints were planed and across the grain.

2nd Experiment.—The segmented arch, Fig. 13 was next tried with the eccentric load.

A short needle was thrust in voussoir 2 on the left, in the direction of the vertical through its centre of gravity, as shown in Fig. 24: the arch balanced with 5.4 voussoirs on the top of this needle.

We form the following tables:

RIGHT SIDE.

	s	m	S	M	C
1	1	2.03	1	2.03	2.03
2	1	5.90	2	7.93	3.96
3	1	9.38	3	17·31	5.77
4	1	12.11	4	29.42	7.37
	4	29.42			

LEFT SIDE.

	S	M	S	M	C
1	1.	2.03	1.	2.03	2.03
2	6.4	37.76	7.4	39.79	5.38
3	1.	9.38	8.4	49.17	5.85
4	1.	12.11	9.4	61.28	6.52
	9.4	61.28			

The voussoir on which the weignt was placed would have slid along its joints, but for pins being thrust into its edges in a manner that did not interfere with rotation.

The arch flew out at joint 2 on the right, hence a curve of pressures was tried passing .2 from the inner edge of this joint as also the middle of the crown, and .2 from the intrados at joint 4 on the left. This curve indicated the true curve more closely. A curve of pressures was next tried passing .2 distant from the intrados at joint 4 on the left and the extradosal edge at joints 1 on the left and 4 on the right. In this case we find from the drawing and the tables :

$g_1 = 12.32 \qquad g_3 = 4.14 \qquad g_2 = 14.17$

$a_1 = 5.80 \qquad a_3 = 2.21 \qquad a_2 = 6.8$

$h_1 = 9.$	$h_3 = 0.8$	$h_2 = 9.$
$P_1 = 9.4$	$P_3 = 1.0$	$P_2 = 4.$
$e_1 = 8.2$	$e_3 = 0$	$e_2 = 8.2$
$d_1 = 18.41$	$d_3 = 26.49$	$d_2 = 8.08$

From equations (8), (9) and (10) we obtain

$$P = \frac{5.8 \times 8.2 \times 9.4 - 6.8 \times 8.2 \times 4 + 2.21 \times 0 \times 1}{8.2 \times 26.49} = 1.03$$

$$Q = \frac{5.8 \times 18.41 \times 9.4 + 6.8 \times 8.08 \times 4 - 2.21 \times 26.49}{8.2 \times 26.49 - 0}$$

$$= 5.36$$

$$q = 9 - \frac{5.8 \times 9.4 - 12.32 \times 1.03}{5.36} = 1.2$$

On constructing the curve of pressures with this data, we find that it passes .15 from the intrados at joint 2 on the right and of course .2 distant from the edges at joints 4, 1 and 4, as assumed; hence the true curve will probably pass about .18 from these edges. This is nearly (.03 difference) what we obtained, for the limits from the edges of the line of pressures in the 11th Exp., Fig. 13. The thrust on joint 1 on the left is inclined 16°.5 to the normal to the joint, nearly what we found before. This sliding in this and the last experiment only occurred just before the balancing weight was applied; the line of pressures travelling down the crown joint as the weight was increased, until finally the direction of the pressure on joint 1 exceeded the complement of the angle of friction.

After patiently investigating all the preceding experiments, we can not but conclude that Dr. Scheffler's theory of the curve of pressures, viz., that it corresponds to the minimum thrust that is consistent with the physical properties of the materials, is proved and beautifully illustrated by them.

13. Analytical formulas for arches are founded upon this hypothesis*: that a curve drawn tangent to the resultant pressures on the joints, coincides, for all purposes of testing the stability of the arch, with the line of pressures of Dr. Scheffler.

Now it is evident in the first place that the above hypothesis can only be proved by

---

*Rankine's Civil Engineering, Art. 280.

innumerable graphic constructions; hence the latter method is the real foundation of the first, if the hypothesis is shown to be correct by the constructions. In the second place, the hypothesis is near enough in some cases as *e. g.*, our viaduct, Figs. 9, 10 and 21, but that it is not so in other cases may be seen by drawing the tangent curve to the resultants, in the case of the oval of the Neuilly bridge (Scheffler Fig. II.) about joints 6 and 7 ; the pointed arch, Fig. IV., at joints 4 and 5 ; as also the experiments with the Gothic arches of this article, where the tangent curve does not cut the springing joints at the true centres of pressure, and hence the true line of pressures would not have been given by the analytical formulas. In fact an arch may be perfectly stable, when this tangent curve passes outside of the arch ring. Dr. Scheffler handles this and other theories with gloves off. The graphic method is so simple, and so little liable to error, compared with the other, that constructors will probably prefer it in testing the stability of an arch. It must not be forgotten, though, that analysis has afforded us the proper form of arch for many particular kinds of load ; though the graphic method will effect the same thing by assuming our arch, drawing a line of pressures through the middle of the crown and abutment joints and then taking this line for the centre of the arch. A second approximation will rarely be needed if the first form of arch is chosen with some discretion.

The graphic method is *general* and applies to any conceivable arch, loaded in any conceivable way, symmetrically or otherwise.

The theory of groined and cloistered arches, as well as domes, is treated by Dr. Scheffler, making use of the principle of the least resistance to ascertain their stability.

*** *Any book in this Catalogue sent free by mail on receipt of price.*

VALUABLE
SCIENTIFIC BOOKS,

PUBLISHED BY

D. VAN NOSTRAND,

23 MURRAY STREET AND 27 WARREN STREET,

NEW YORK.

FRANCIS. Lowell Hydraulic Experiments, being a selection from Experiments on Hydraulic Motors, on the Flow of Water over Weirs, in Open Canals of Uniform Rectangular Section, and through submerged Orifices and diverging Tubes. Made at Lowell, Massachusetts. By James B. Francis, C. E. 2d edition, revised and enlarged, with many new experiments, and illustrated with twenty-three copperplate engravings. 1 vol. 4to, cloth......................$15 00

ROEBLING (J. A.) Long and Short Span Railway Bridges. By John A. Roebling, C. E. Illustrated with large copperplate engravings of plans and views. Imperial folio, cloth.............................. 25 00

CLARKE (T. C.) Description of the Iron Railway Bridge over the Mississippi River, at Quincy, Illinois. Thomas Curtis Clarke, Chief Engineer. Illustrated with 21 lithographed plans. 1 vol. 4to, cloth.. 7 50

TUNNER (P.) A Treatise on Roll-Turning for the Manufacture of Iron. By Peter Tunner. Translated and adapted by John B. Pearse, of the Pennsylvania Steel Works, with numerous engravings wood cuts and folio atlas of plates.................. $10 00

ISHERWOOD (B. F.) Engineering Precedents for Steam Machinery. Arranged in the most practical and useful manner for Engineers. By B. F. Isherwood, Civil Engineer, U. S. Navy. With Illustrations. Two volumes in one. 8vo, cloth........... $2 50

BAUERMAN. Treatise on the Metallurgy of Iron, containing outlines of the History of Iron Manufacture, methods of Assay, and analysis of Iron Ores, processes of manufacture of Iron and Steel, etc., etc. By H. Bauerman. First American edition. Revised and enlarged, with an Appendix on the Martin Process for making Steel, from the report of Abram S. Hewitt. Illustrated with numerous wood engravings. 12mo, cloth.................................... 2 00

CAMPIN on the Construction of Iron Roofs. By Francis Campin. 8vo, with plates, cloth........... 3 00

COLLINS. The Private Book of Useful Alloys and Memoranda for Goldsmiths, Jewellers, &c. By James E. Collins. 18mo, cloth.................... 75

CIPHER AND SECRET LETTER AND TELEGRAPHIC CODE, with Hogg's Improvements. The most perfect secret code ever invented or discovered. Impossible to read without the key. By C. S. Larrabee. 18mo, cloth. 1 00

COLBURN. The Gas Works of London. By Zerah Colburn, C. E. 1 vol 12mo, boards............... 60

CRAIG (B. F.) Weights and Measures. An account of the Decimal System, with Tables of Conversion for Commercial and Scientific Uses. By B. F. Craig, M.D. 1 vol. square 32mo, limp cloth.... 50

NUGENT. Treatise on Optics; or, Light and Sight, theoretically and practically treated; with the application to Fine Art and Industrial Pursuits. By E. Nugent. With one hundred and three illustrations. 12mo, cloth...................................... 2 00

GLYNN (J.) Treatise on the Power of Water, as applied to drive Flour Mills, and to give motion to Turbines and other Hydrostatic Engines. By Joseph

Glynn. Third edition, revised and enlarged, with numerous illustrations. 12mo, cloth. $1 00

HUMBER. A Handy Book for the Calculation of Strains in Girders and similar Structures, and their Strength, consisting of Formulæ and corresponding Diagrams, with numerous details for practical application. By William Humber. 12mo, fully illustrated, cloth.................................... 2 50

GRUNER. The Manufacture of Steel. By M. L. Gruner. Translated from the French, by Lenox Smith, with an appendix on the Bessamer process in the United States, by the translator. Illustrated by Lithographed drawings and wood cuts. 8vo, cloth.. 3 50

AUCHINCLOSS. Link and Valve Motions Simplified. Illustrated with 37 wood-cuts, and 21 lithographic plates, together with a Travel Scale, and numerous useful Tables. By W. S. Auchincloss. 8vo, cloth.. 3 00

VAN BUREN. Investigations of Formulas, for the strength of the Iron parts of Steam Machinery. By J. D. Van Buren, Jr., C. E. Illustrated, 8vo, cloth. 2 00

JOYNSON. Designing and Construction of Machine Gearing. Illustrated, 8vo, cloth.................. 2 00

GILLMORE. Coignet Beton and other Artificial Stone. By Q. A. Gillmore, Major U. S. Corps Engineers. 9 plates, views, &c. 8vo, cloth.................... 2 50

SAELTZER. Treattse on Acoustics in connection with Ventilation. By Alexander Saeltzer, Architect. 12mo, cloth.................................... 2 00

THE EARTH'S CRUST. A handy Outline of Geology. By David Page. Illustrated, 18mo, cloth.... 75

DICTIONARY of Manufactures, Mining, Machinery, and the Industrial Arts. By George Dodd. 12mo, cloth.. 2 00

FRANCIS. On the Strength of Cast-Iron Pillars, with Tables for the use of Engineers, Architects, and Builders. By James B. Francis, Civil Engineer. 1 vol. 8vo, cloth................................ 2 00

GILLMORE (Gen. Q. A.) Treatise on Limes, Hydraulic Cements, and Mortars. Papers on Practical Engineering, U. S. Engineer Department, No. 9, containing Reports of numerous Experiments conducted in New York City, during the years 1858 to 1861, inclusive. By Q. A. Gillmore, Bvt. Maj -Gen., U. S. A., Major, Corps of Engineers. With numerous illustrations. 1 vol, 8vo, cloth............... $4 00

HARRISON. The Mechanic's Tool Book, with Practical Rules and Suggestions for Use of Machinists, Iron Workers, and others. By W. B. Harrison, associate editor of the "American Artisan." Illustrated with 44 engravings. 12mo, cloth........... 1 50

HENRICI (Olaus). Skeleton Structures, especially in their application to the Building of Steel and Iron Bridges. By Olaus Henrici. With folding plates and diagrams. 1 vol. 8vo, cloth.................... 3 00

HEWSON (Wm.) Principles and Practice of Embanking Lands from River Floods, as applied to the Levees of the Mississippi. By William Hewson, Civil Engineer. 1 vol. 8vo, cloth....................... 2 00

HOLLEY (A. L.) Railway Practice. American and European Railway Practice, in the economical Generation of Steam, including the Materials and Construction of Coal-burning Boilers, Combustion, the Variable Blast, Vaporization, Circulation, Superheating, Supplying and Heating Feed-water, etc., and the Adaptation of Wood and Coke-burning Engines to Coal-burning; and in Permanent Way, including Road-bed, Sleepers, Rails, Joint-fastenings, Street Railways, etc., etc. By Alexander L. Holley, B. P. With 77 lithographed plates. 1 vol. folio, cloth.... 12 00

KING (W. H.) Lessons and Practical Notes on Steam, the Steam Engine, Propellers, etc., etc., for Young Marine Engineers, Students, and others. By the late W. H. King, U. S. Navy. Revised by Chief Engineer J. W. King, U. S. Navy. Twelfth edition, enlarged. 8vo, cloth. 2 00

MINIFIE (Wm.) Mechanical Drawing. A Text-Book of Geometrical Drawing for the use of Mechanics and Schools, in which the Definitions and Rules of Geometry are familiarly explained; the Practical Problems are arranged, from the most simple to the more complex, and in their description technicalities are avoided as much as possible. With illustrations for Drawing Plans, Sections, and Elevations of Railways and Machinery; an Introduction to Isometrical Drawing, and an Essay on Linear Perspective and Shadows. Illustrated with over 200 diagrams engraved on steel. By Wm. Minifie, Architect. Seventh edition. With an Appendix on the Theory and Application of Colors. 1 vol. 8vo, cloth............ $4 00

"It is the best work on Drawing that we have ever seen, and is especially a text-book of Geometrical Drawing for the use of Mechanics and Schools. No young Mechanic, such as a Machinists, Engineer, Cabinet-maker, Millwright, or Carpenter, should be without it."—*Scientific American.*

—— Geometrical Drawing. Abridged from the octavo edition, for the use of Schools. Illustrated with 48 steel plates. Fifth edition. 1 vol. 12mo, cloth.... 2 00

STILLMAN (Paul.) Steam Engine Indicator, and the Improved Manometer Steam and Vacuum Gauges—their Utility and Application. By Paul Stillman. New edition. 1 vol. 12mo, flexible cloth........... 1 00

SWEET (S. H.) Special Report on Coal; showing its Distribution, Classification, and cost delivered over different routes to various points in the State of New York, and the principal cities on the Atlantic Coast. By S. H. Sweet. With maps, 1 vol. 8vo, cloth..... 3 00

WALKER (W. H.) Screw Propulsion. Notes on Screw Propulsion: its Rise and History. By Capt. W. H. Walker, U. S. Navy. 1 vol. 8vo, cloth..... 75

WARD (J. H.) Steam for the Million. A popular Treatise on Steam and its Application to the Useful Arts, especially to Navigation. By J. H. Ward, Commander U. S. Navy. New and revised edition. 1 vol. 8vo, cloth................................. 1 00

WEISBACH (Julius). Principles of the Mechanics of Machinery and Engineering. By Dr. Julius Weisbach, of Freiburg. Translated from the last German edition. Vol. I., 8vo, cloth.. .... 10 00

DIEDRICH. The Theory of Strains, a Compendium for the calculation and construction of Bridges, Roofs, and Cranes, with the application of Trigonometrical Notes, containing the most comprehensive information in regard to the Resulting strains for a permanent Load, as also for a combined (Permanent and Rolling) Load. In two sections, adadted to the requirements of the present time. By John Diedrich, C. E. Illustrated by numerous plates and diagrams. 8vo, cloth.................................... 5 00

WILLIAMSON (R. S.) On the use of the Barometer on Surveys and Reconnoissances. Part I. Meteorology in its Connection with Hypsometry. Part II. Barometric Hypsometry. By R. S. Wiliamson, Bvt. Lieut.-Col. U. S. A., Major Corps of Engineers. With Illustrative Tables and Engravings. Paper No. 15, Professional Papers, Corps of Engineers. 1 vol. 4to, cloth... .... 15 00

POOK (S. M.) Method of Comparing the Lines and Draughting Vessels Propelled by Sail or Steam. Including a chapter on Laying off on the Mould-Loft Floor. By Samuel M. Pook, Naval Constructor. 1 vol. 8vo, with illustrations, cloth........... 5 00

ALEXANDER (J. H.) Universal Dictionary of Weights and Measures, Ancient and Modern, reduced to the standards of the United States of America. By J. H. Alexander. New edition, enlarged. 1 vol. 8vo, cloth 3 50

BROOKLYN WATER WORKS. Containing a Descriptive Account of the Construction of the Works, and also Reports on the Brooklyn, Hartford, Belleville and Cambridge Pumping Engines. With illustrations. 1 vol. folio, cloth..........................

RICHARDS' INDICATOR. A Treatise on the Richards Steam Engine Indicator, with an Appendix by F. W. Bacon, M. E. 18mo, flexible, cloth......... 1 00

POPE. Modern Practice of the Electric Telegraph. A Hand Book for Electricians and operators. By Frank L. Pope. Eighth edition, revised and enlarged, and fully illustrated. 8vo, cloth.......................... $2.00

"There is no other work of this kind in the English language that contains in so small a compass so much practical information in the application of galvanic electricity to telegraphy. It should be in the hands of every one interested in telegraphy, or the use of Batteries for other purposes."

MORSE. Examination of the Telegraphic Apparatus and the Processes in Telegraphy. By Samuel F. Morse, LL.D., U. S. Commissioner Paris Universal Exposition, 1867. Illustrated, 8vo, cloth.......... $2 00

SABINE. History and Progress of the Electric Telegraph, with descriptions of some of the apparatus. By Robert Sabine, C. E. Second edition, with additions, 12mo, cloth............................... 1 25

CULLEY. A Hand-Book of Practical Telegraphy. By R. S. Culley, Engineer to the Electric and International Telegraph Company. Fourth edition, revised and enlarged. Illustrated 8vo, cloth.............. 5 00

BENET. Electro-Ballistic Machines, and the Schultz Chronoscope. By Lieut.-Col. S. V. Benet, Captain of Ordnance, U. S. Army. Illustrated, second edition, 4to, cloth................................ 3 00

MICHAELIS. The Le Boulenge Chronograph, with three Lithograph folding plates of illustrations. By Brevet Captain O. E. Michaelis, First Lieutenant Ordnance Corps, U. S. Army, 4to, cloth.......... 3 00

ENGINEERING FACTS AND FIGURES An Annual Register of Progress in Mechanical Engineering and Construction, for the years 1863, 64, 65, 66, 67, 68. Fully illustrated, 6 vols. 18mo, cloth, $2.50 per vol., each volume sold separately..............

HAMILTON. Useful Information for Railway Men. Compiled by W. G. Hamilton, Engineer. Fifth edition, revised and enlarged, 562 pages Pocket form. Morocco, gilt.................................... 2 00

STUART. The Civil and Military Engineers of America. By Gen. C. B. Stuart. With 9 finely executed portraits of eminent engineers, and illustrated by engravings of some of the most important works constructed in America. 8vo, cloth.................. $5 00

STONEY. The Theory of Strains in Girders and similar structures, with observations on the application of Theory to Practice, and Tables of Strength and other properties of Materials. By Bindon B. Stoney, B. A. New and revised edition, enlarged, with numerous engravings on wood, by Oldham. Royal 8vo, 664 pages. Complete in one volume. 8vo, cloth....... 15 00

SHREVE. A Treatise on the Strength of Bridges and Roofs. Comprising the determination of Algebraic formulas for strains in Horizontal, Inclined or Rafter, Triangular, Bowstring, Lenticular and other Trusses, from fixed and moving loads, with practical applications and examples, for the use of Students and Engineers. By Samuel H. Shreve, A. M., Civil Engineer. 87 wood cut illustrations. 8vo, cloth............... 5 00

MERRILL. Iron Truss Bridges for Railroads. The method of calculating strains in Trusses, with a careful comparison of the most prominent Trusses, in reference to economy in combination, etc., etc. By Brevet. Col. William E. Merrill, U. S. A., Major Corps of Engineers, with nine lithographed plates of Illustrations. 4to, cloth........................ 5 00

WHIPPLE. An Elementary and Practical Treatise on Bridge Building. An enlarged and improved edition of the author's original work. By S. Whipple, C. E., inventor of the Whipple Bridges, &c. Illustrated 8vo, cloth.. 4 00

THE KANSAS CITY BRIDGE. With an account of the Regimen of the Missouri River, and a description of the methods used for Founding in that River. By O. Chanute, Chief Engineer, and George Morrison, Assistant Engineer. Illustrated with five lithographic views and twelve plates of plans. 4to, cloth, 6 00

www.ingramcontent.com/pod-product-compliance
Lightning Source LLC
LaVergne TN
LVHW021421110826
845150LV00007B/2018

* 9 7 8 1 4 2 5 5 0 9 1 7 0 *